THE GOLDEN YEARS OF
WELSH
RUGBY

GARETH EDWARDS

THE GOLDEN YEARS OF
WELSH
RUGBY

GARETH EDWARDS

Edited by
David Parry-Jones

Additional commentary by
J. P. R. Williams
Barry John
Gerald Davies
Phil Bennett
and Mervyn Davies

Harrap London

First published in Great Britain 1982
by HARRAP LIMITED
19–23 Ludgate Hill, London EC4M 7PD

ISBN 0 245-53836-4

Designed by Michael R. Carter

Printed and bound in Great Britain
by Robert Hartnoll, Bodmin

Contents

Preface

I was fortunate enough to play International rugby football during what people describe as a golden era of the game in Wales.

Points were piled up, records fell, crowds thronged to see us play and roar their appreciation.

Now five team-mates and I have put our heads together and looked back on the days when we wore the red jersey and its three proud feathers.

Two stand-off halves in Barry John and Phil Bennett, full-back J. P. R. Williams, wing Gerald Davies and iron-hard number 8 forward Mervyn Davies join me to reflect on the moments that mattered to Welsh rugby between 1966 when Barry and Gerald won their first caps and 1979 when J.P.R. led Wales for the last time.

Occasionally we tumbled from grace — when the enemy was New Zealand, for example, or the venue Dublin. But for the most part our efforts were crowned with success.

What is more, I think we can claim to have won well. That is to say, we players enjoyed ourselves and at the same time gave pleasure to millions of spectators who watched us in the world's great rugby arenas and on their television screens.

I hope that this book will serve to commemorate endeavours whose afterglow is indeed tinged with gold.

Gareth Edwards

HRH Prince Charles makes his first public appearance as Prince of Wales. He is with captain Brian Price before the Wales v Ireland match, 1969.

9

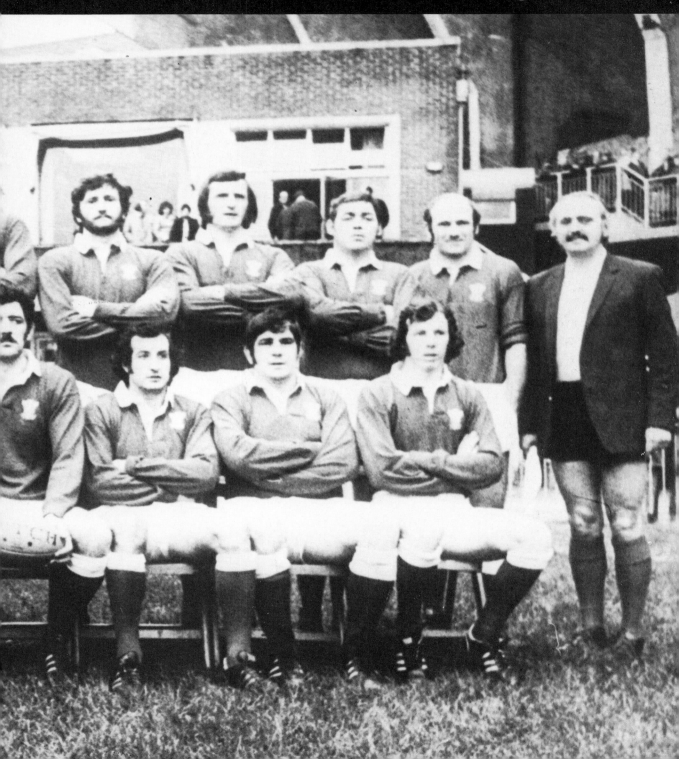

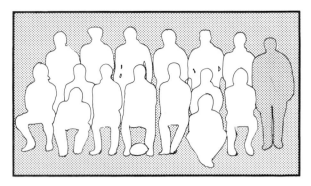

WALES XV v ENGLAND, 1971: *Back row, left to right:* D. B. Llewelyn (Lanelli), T. M. Davies (London Welsh), M. G. Roberts (London Welsh), D. Williams (Ebbw Vale), W. D. Thomas (Llanelli), W. D. Morris (Neath). *Seated, left to right:* J. P. R. Williams (London Welsh), J. C. Bevan (Cardiff), B. John (Cardiff), S. J. Dawes (London Welsh – Captain), J. Taylor (London Welsh), G. O. Edwards (Cardiff), T. G. R. Davies (London Welsh). *On ground:* J. Young (Harrogate), A. J. Lewis (Ebbw Vale).

WALES XV v ENGLAND 1975: *Back row, left to right:* S. P. Fenwick (Bridgend), G. Price (Pontypool), G. A. D. Wheel (Swansea), A. J. Martin (Aberavon), R. W. R. Gravell (Llanelli), T. P. Evans (Swansea), A. G. Faulkner (Pontypool), T. J. Cobner (Pontypool). *Seated, left to right:* T. G. R. Davies (Cardiff), J. P. R. Williams (London Welsh), J. D. Bevan (Aberavon), T. M. Davies (Swansea – Captain), G. O. Edwards (Cardiff), R. W. Windsor (Pontypool), J. J. Williams (Llanelli).

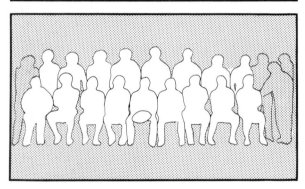

WALES XV v SCOTLAND 1978: *Back row, left to right:* G. Price (Pontypool), J. Squire (Pontypool), D. Quinnell (Llanelli), A. J. Martin (Aberavon), G. A. D. Wheel (Swansea), A. G. Faulkner (Pontypool), T. J. Cobner (Pontypool). *Seated, left to right:* R. W. R. Gravell (Llanelli), T. G. R. Davies (Cardiff), J. P. R. Williams (Bridgend), P. Bennett (Llanelli – Captain), G. O. Edwards (Cardiff), R. W. Windsor (Pontypool), J. J. Williams (Llanelli), S. P. Fenwick (Bridgend).

Subdue and penetrate: the pragmatic approach which made possible a golden era in Welsh rugby. Here Derek Quinnell is its fearsome embodiment.

THE GOLDEN YEARS OF
WELSH RUGBY

THE MATCHES

3 December 1966 at Cardiff

WALES 11 (1G 1PG 1T)
AUSTRALIA 14 (1G 1T 1DG 1PG)

FACT BOX

In this fourth encounter between the two nations Delme Thomas and Ken Braddock won first caps in addition to Barry John and Gerald Davies. But tearaway flanker Haydn Morgan played his last game for Wales.

Wales T. G. Price (Llanelli), S. J. Watkins (Newport), S. J. Dawes (L. Welsh), T. G. R. Davies (Cardiff), D. I. E. Bebb (Swansea), B. John (Llanelli), A. R. Lewis (Abertillery), D. Williams (Ebbw Vale), N. R. Gale (Llanelli), D. J. Lloyd (Bridgend), B. Price (Newport), W. D. Thomas (Llanelli), K. J. Braddock (Newbridge), A. E. I. Pask (Abertillery, Captain), H. J. Morgan (Abertillery).

Australia J. K. Lenehan, E. S. Boyce, R. J. Marks, J. E. Brass, A. M. Cardy, P. F. Hawthorne, K. W. Catchpole (Captain), J. M. Miller, P. G. Johnson, A. R. Miller, R. G. Teitzel, R. J. Heming, M. P. Purcell, J. F. O'Gorman, G. V. Davis.

SCORERS
Wales *Tries* — Morgan, Dawes; *Con.* — T. Price; *Pen.* — T. Price.
Australia *Tries* — Lenehan, Cardy; *Con.* — Hawthorne; *Pen.* — Lenehan; *D.G.* — Hawthorne.

Referee: K. D. Kelleher (IRFU).

Gerald Davies's blistering pace sends the Wallaby defence to panic stations. But later it was the Welsh who had that sinking feeling.

Wales's Trial match had been a momentous affair. The Easterners on the terraces shouted the name of the reigning stand-off half David Watkins — and the West roared back 'Barry John!'

In the event the latter, a college student who hailed from Cefneithin in Carmarthenshire, became the selectors' choice to partner Allan Lewis of Abertillery against the touring Wallabies at Cardiff Arms Park. Among the other new caps was Thomas Gerald Reames Davies, now of Cardiff RFC but raised in another Carmarthenshire village, Llansaint.

An age of great players, and great achievements, had opened.

Not with a bang, however — rather a whimper. On their debuts the two newcomers, destined to exercise a profound influence on world rugby in years to come, were part of an experiment which failed. In an attempt to match the tourists' flair, Wales abandoned the tight, calculating approach that had brought success in recent seasons. But they lacked the generalship at stand-off half to make new, more fluent tactics pay off.

BARRY JOHN: There was no squad preparation in those days. No one had bothered to give me encouragement or advice of any kind. So, overeager to get everything right, I passed the ball when I should have kicked, and vice versa.

I must have looked really raw — and that's a shame, because this was not a tremendously demanding game. A season or two later I could have taken complete control of it.

Early on I made a good break but, unfortunately, mistimed what should have been a scoring pass. A certain try went begging.

Soon, however, a chip by John to the left corner was gathered by wing Dewi Bebb, who put Haydn Morgan over for an unconverted try. Brave Phil Hawthorne, who played through much of the match with a depressed fracture of the cheekbone, dropped an equalizing goal, and then there was an exchange of penalties between Terry Price and Jim Lenehan. The latter, who came from full-back to join his three-quarters frequently, next scored a try which he could not convert at the corner flag to give Australia the lead.

The visitors knew they had made sure of a first-ever win over Wales when the home side began desperately running the ball in their own 25-area.

GERALD DAVIES: I got the ball and my opposite number Dick Marks — a big, heavy man — at one and the same time. His tackle allowed Australia to gain possession, and by the time I had got to my feet Cardy was crossing for a try near the corner flag. Hawthorne converted, and we were all left with that sinking feeling.

John Dawes's injury-time try, converted by Terry Price, could do no more than lift Wales to double figures and respectability.

GERALD DAVIES: The biggest impression on me was made by the Australian half backs. At the time, British rugby was obsessed with 'good ball' which the forwards were directed to supply. Speed was sacrificed for accuracy. But Catchpole and Hawthorne made nonsense of this idea. They pounced on anything and everything the Wallaby pack sent back. Hence the midfield got the ball early, with plenty of time and space. Wings Cardy and Boyce saw a lot of it, too.

MATCH 2

4 February 1967 at Murrayfield

SCOTLAND 11 (1G 1T 1DG)
WALES 5 (1G)

FACT BOX

Stuart Watkins's try was his eighth for Wales in 13 games. By converting it full back Terry Price became his country's third highest post-War scorer with 37 points.

Scotland S. Wilson, A. J. W. Hinshelwood, J. W. C. Turner, B. M. Simmers, D. J. Whyte, D. H. Chisholm, A. J. Hastie, J. D. MacDonald, F. A. L. Laidlaw, D. M. D. Rollo, P. K. Stagg, W. J. Hunter, D. Grant, J. W. Telfer, J. P. Fisher (Captain).

Wales T. G. Price (L. Welsh), S. J. Watkins (Newport), W. H. Raybould (L. Welsh), T. G. R. Davies (Cardiff), D. I. E. Bebb (Swansea), B. John (Llanelli), W. Hullin (Cardiff), D. J. Lloyd (Bridgend), B. I. Rees (L. Welsh), J. P. O'Shea (Cardiff), B. Price (Newport), W. T. Mainwaring (Aberavon), K. J. Braddock (Newbridge), A. E. I. Pask (Abertillery, Captain), J. Taylor (L. Welsh).

SCORERS
Scotland *Tries* – Hinshelwood, Telfer; *Con.* – Wilson; *D.G.* – Chisholm.
Wales *Try* – Watkins; *Con.* – T. Price.

Referee: K. D. Kelleher (IRFU).

In radical mood, the Welsh selectors performed major surgery upon their team for Edinburgh, where experienced men like Allan Lewis and Norman Gale were sidelined to permit the introduction of six new caps. Longest surviving of them was to be the almost unknown John Taylor, brought up in Watford but of lineage which permitted him to join London Welsh RFC.

Gerald Davies and Barry John held their places — but there was speculation about the latter's fitness.

BARRY JOHN: Three days before my first appearance at Murrayfield I was hobbling around Trinity College Carmarthen on a stick!

During the Final Trial match I had suffered a knee injury necessitating thirteen stitches and, even when it was mending, the surrounding skin remained taut and painful. I should have withdrawn from the Welsh team.

The trouble was, I feared that David Watkins might be reinstated and play well enough to keep his place. Perhaps this was understandable in a young man — but also it was very stupid and, predictably, I completely failed to do myself justice in Edinburgh.

Despite the 6 ft 7 in presence of Peter Stagg among the Scottish forwards, the Welsh managed to control the first-half exchanges, and even gain a 5–0 lead. Stuart Watkins got possession from a short line-out and slipped through the defence for a corner try which Terry Price converted magnificently.

It may be, however, that the visitors were inhibited after the failure of their running game with the Wallabies. Soon after the interval the Scots sensed that they might move the ball profitably against hesitant defenders. Full-back Stewart Wilson saw a chance to join his three-quarters, drew in Dewi Bebb, and sent Hinshelwood flying in for an unconverted try.

BARRY JOHN: That finished me! The impact of Sandy Hinshelwood's dive for the line beat my attempted cover tackle and spun me round; my knee struck the wooden corner flag and the wound promptly opened up again.

Scots full back Stewart Wilson fails to prevent Stuart Watkins giving Wales the lead with a try at the corner.

A kick into the box by scrum half Bill Hullin. But after Wales's defeat he lost the selectors' confidence.

Soon, to an endless roar from the terraces, Scotland forced their opponents to concede a five-yard scrummage, from which David Chisholm dropped a goal to inch his side ahead.

The home team's tails were now up, and when Wales scrum-half Billy Hullin failed to gather a loose ball on his own goal-line Alex Hastie intervened smartly. He found support from number 8 forward Jim Telfer, who burst over for a decisive try which Wilson converted to end the scoring.

GERALD DAVIES: From the first, I have enjoyed playing at Murrayfield. The turf is springy and, probably because the main terrace is open to the sky, there is a feeling of acres of space waiting to be used.

However, we had lost — and we knew that there were bound to be changes. Barry John and Billy Hullin lost their places for the Irish match, and I felt relief at my retention. Once you have had a taste of International rugby in Wales, you desperately want more!

BARRY JOHN: Back in Carmarthen after our defeat I avoided people who had seen me limping beforehand. Fans will forgive a player who has an off-day; but not one who lets his team down through foolishness.

11 March 1967 at Cardiff

WALES   0
IRELAND 3 (1T)

The Welsh pack are no match for Ireland's fiery eight. Here **Allan Lewis** *(right)* **tries to tidy up as Ken Goodall comes through on the rampage.**

FACT BOX

For the first time in 16 games the Welsh failed to score — and for the first time in the 20th century were unable to score against Ireland at Cardiff! Alun Pask won the last of his 26 consecutive caps.

Wales   G. T. R. Hodgson (Neath), S. J. Watkins (Newport), W. H. Raybould (L. Welsh), T. G. R. Davies (Cardiff), D. I. E. Bebb (Swansea), D. Watkins (Newport, Captain), A. R. Lewis (Abertillery), J. P. O'Shea (Cardiff), B. I. Rees (L. Welsh), D. J. Lloyd (Bridgend), W. T. Mainwaring (Aberavon), B. Price (Newport), K. J. Braddock (Newbridge), A. E. I. Pask (Abertillery), J. Taylor (L. Welsh).

Ireland   T. J. Kiernan, A. T. A. Duggan, F. P. K. Bresnihan, J. C. Walsh, N. H. Brophy, C. M. H. Gibson, R. M. Young, S. McHale, K. W. Kennedy, S. A. Hutton, W. J. McBride, M. G. Molloy, N. A. Murphy (Captain), K. G. Goodall, M. G. Doyle.

SCORERS
Ireland   *Try* — Duggan.

Referee: M. H. Titcomb (RFU).

David Watkins could scarcely believe his ears when he heard the Welsh team chosen to meet Ireland. Not only had the selectors brought him back in place of Barry John at stand-off half (to partner his British Lions colleague Allan Lewis) — they had also given him the captaincy, relieving number 8 forward Alun Pask of the responsibility. Watkins was also the twenty-third player to be called upon in just three matches, which so far had seen nine changes.

BARRY JOHN: Not only had I played poorly as an individual at Murrayfield — I had also failed to hit it off with Billy Hullin, whose pass reached me at a wholly unsuitable angle and velocity. So I had been expecting to be dropped, and sat resignedly on the reserves' bench to watch David Watkins's come-back game.

I could not learn much from him, since our ways of playing the game were poles apart. But he was undeniably a fine stand-off half, in the explosive style of a Cliff Morgan or Phil Bennett. I thought of him as a 'counter-puncher' — that is, he waited for tacklers to commit themselves and then — pfft! — he was gone. He could be contained by a cautious stifling of his options, but one lapse of concentration by defenders usually proved fatal.

Ireland included twelve of the team which had rudely interrupted Wales's Triple Crown progress a year earlier in Dublin, plus a new number 8 forward of great promise in the Newcastle University student Ken Goodall. They found top gear immedi-

ately: the pack won possession within their opponents' 25-area, where mercurial Mike Gibson raced back towards strength. Supporting prop Sam Hutton managed to smuggle the ball to Roger Young, who rifled out a swift pass which gave Jerry Walsh in the centre time to weigh the tactical options. He chose a chip to the right corner, where Alan Duggan grasped the bouncing ball and sped past Dewi Bebb for a sparkling unconverted try. Although the game was but three minutes old, it was to be the winning score.

For the remaining 77 minutes Wales experienced only frustration. At forward the fiery visitors, led with inspiration by Noel Murphy, were much too strong for a home pack which often saw its isolated ball-winning efforts nullified by Roger Young's non-stop harassment of Allan Lewis. Away from the scrummages a gale-force wind defeated the Welsh backs' attempts to bring fluency to their play.

Later on, in a desperate attempt to pull the game from the fire, David Watkins scattered the defence with a typical side-stepping burst at top speed. But, with the line beckoning and the crowd howling for a score, the Newport man's ankle was tapped by the covering Goodall. Ireland regrouped, and the final whistle sounded.

3 April 1967 at Stade Colombes
FRANCE 20 (1G 2T 2DG 1PG)
WALES 14 (1G 1DG 2PG)

FACT BOX

The Welsh defeat was their fourth in a row — a sorry sequence that had not occurred since the 1924–25 season.
Ron Jones is the only member of Coventry RFC to have been capped by Wales.

France J. Gachassin, M. Arnaudet, C. Dourthe, J-P. Lux, C. Darrouy (Captain), G. Camberabero, L. Camberabero, A. Gruarin, J-M. Cabanier, J-C. Berejnoi, E. Cester, J. Fort, M. Sitjar, B. Dauga, C. Carrere.

Wales T. G. Price (L. Welsh), S. J. Watkins (Newport), W. H. Raybould (L. Welsh), T. G. R. Davies (Cardiff), D. I. E. Bebb (Swansea), D. Watkins (Newport, Captain), G. O. Edwards (Cardiff), D. Williams (Ebbw Vale), B. I. Rees (L. Welsh), D. J. Lloyd (Bridgend), B. Price (Newport), W. T. Mainwaring (Aberavon), R. E. Jones (Coventry), W. D. Morris (Neath), J. Taylor (L. Welsh).

SCORERS
France *Tries* – G. Camberabero, Dauga, Dourthe; *Con.* – G. Camberabero; *Pen.* – G. Camberabero; *D.G.* – G. Camberabero (2).
Wales *Try* – Bebb; *Con.* – T. Price; *Pens.* – T. Price (2); *D.G.* – D. Watkins.

Referee: P. d'Arcy (IRFU).

Not only did the band fail to play the Welsh anthem — it struck up *God Save the Queen* instead! Thus did the arrival upon the International scene of the great Gareth Edwards take place without an uplifting fanfare.

The youngster from Gwaun-cae-Gurwen, however, had other than melodic thoughts on his mind as he trotted from the tunnel up into the seething, screeching Colombes stadium. One of a trio of new caps (along with Ron Jones of Coventry RFC and

Dai Morris of Neath), he was the third scrum-half to be used by Wales during a season that had become a nightmare. In the last decade, moreover, his country had found it increasingly hard to win in Paris.

In these circumstances Edwards, schooled at Pontardawe and Millfield and by now a student at Cardiff Training College, sensibly kept a low profile and acquitted himself satisfactorily in a Welsh team which, though beaten, did better than expected.

GARETH EDWARDS: For the first game I took confidence from the basic skills developed during my rugby upbringing under the wing of Bill Samuel, the school coach who became my great friend and mentor.

I needed something to cling to, for the pressure was on from all directions — fifteen Frenchmen for a start! There were also numerous scrum-halves back in Wales who

A vital moment on his debut for Gareth Edwards: he prepares to deliver his first pass from the base of the scrum. . . . Moments later all was relief and delight.

coveted my number nine jersey, and I feared that a poor display in Paris might persuade the selectors to try Glyn Turner or Gwilym Treharne or Selwyn Williams.

My International debut was smoothed by my getting into the game early. At the first line-out Brian Price won possession, and the ball reached me via Denzil Williams. The 30-yard touch-finder I put in was very important for my morale.

Next came my first pass to David Watkins. The ball travelled no more than five yards, but as I hit the ground I told myself with relief and delight, 'It's there! He's got it!'

Watkins dropped a goal for Wales early on, and Terry Price put over two penalty goals. And at one point the visitors seemed to be heading for an unexpected victory, thanks to magnificent ball-control by Dewi Bebb along the left touch-line which brought him a corner-flag try converted by Price.

But then Guy Camberabero resumed a personal blitz on Welsh hopes. He converted a try by Claude

Dourthe, dropped a goal to restore France's lead, and finally clinched victory for his team by scampering across for a try after Terry Price had fumbled a pass on the Welsh 25-line. The dropped goal and penalty which he had contributed at the outset enabled him to finish with a personal tally of 14 points. By the close France's forwards too had exposed an array of Welsh shortcomings.

GARETH EDWARDS; The game went by in a flash. At the final whistle I stood on the half-way line, a picture of disppointment. But that was not just because we had lost — in my exhilaration I just wanted everyone to carry on playing!

Terry Price finished with eight points, but better kicking could have brought him another half dozen and won the game for us. Late in the game he also dropped a pass that could have brought a try after I had broken the defence.

I shall always be grateful to Dewi Bebb, who smuggled away the match ball under his jersey and gave it to me afterwards as a wonderful souvenir of my first game for Wales.

MATCH 5

15 April 1967 at Cardiff

WALES 34 (5G 1DG 2PG)
ENGLAND 21 (3T 4PG)

To the game's followers, even those dazzled by the glories of the 'seventies, this match still stands out as a beacon, highlighting the very best that the game of rugby football has to offer.

Phil Judd's England team had come to Cardiff hunting a Triple Crown, but in the event were destroyed almost single-handed by new cap Keith Jarrett, a member of Newport RFC who had been at Monmouth School until the previous December. Already recognized as a phenomenal place-kicker, Jarrett hit form with five conversions and two penalty goals, while his try was an unexpected bonus: the first such score by a Welsh full-back since Vivian Jenkins crossed against the Irish in 1934, and only the second in all matches played by Wales.

J. P. R. WILLIAMS: I was in a party of Millfield schoolboys who came to see the game — and I knew it was bound to be Jarrett's day after his first penalty kick went over via an upright.

He had a marvellous game. But I am glad that in subsequent international games he appeared in his proper position of centre. Too often selectors pick a wing or a midfield man at full-back simply because he is a good attacker, whereas the position requires great study and specialization. I see the full-back as primarily his team's last line of defence.

A packed house basking in warm sunshine applauded the first Jarrett penalty, after which Billy Raybould dropped a goal. England hit back with a well-engineered try touched down by Barton, but Jarrett was soon on target again with a penalty and the conversion of Dai Morris's try. The home team led 14–6 at the interval, Roger Hosen having put over a penalty goal for England. Next came Gerald Davies's first try for Wales.

GERALD DAVIES: I gave Dewi Bebb the ball inside our half and stayed with him as he drew England's full-back, Roger Hosen. When the return pass came I still had 40 yards to cover, but I put my head back and managed to reach the line. The conversion was a formality, such was Jarrett's form.

England, however, now crept up to 15–19 with a Keith Savage try and another Hosen penalty. Then, with the crowd becoming apprehensive, Jarrett covered himself with more distinction, and scored one of the most spectacular tries in the annals of rugby football.

A diagonal kick sat up obligingly off the hard turf for the youngster to collect at top speed on the Welsh 10-yard line. Seconds later, as he maintained momentum down the left-hand touchline, it became clear that he would outflank the England cover; and he duly reached the corner flag, breathless after a

60-yard sprint. To a torrent of unbroken applause, the Newport man neatly placed a lengthy conversion.

Although the England challenge was now broken, Jarrett had not yet finished. Inevitably he converted tries by Bebb and — again — Gerald Davies.

GERALD DAVIES: This try was from short range. I beat centre Colin McFadyean on the outside before selling a dummy to his partner, Danny Hearn, and scoring half way between the posts and the corner flag.

Had it not been for Keith Jarrett's display this match might have been remembered for my own performance. It was almost unheard of for a midfield player to score twice in a representative match. But I enjoyed Keith's display so much that I was quite happy to let him bask in the glory.

As Wales eased up the visitors claimed six consolation points through a fourth Hosen penalty and another try by lock Barton. After an unforgettable display it was still Wales's lot to collect the Championship wooden spoon, France clinching the title with a victory over Ireland in Paris.

Wales skipper David Watkins lines up a tactical kick for his three quarters. Soon the Newport pivot with the electric heels would announce his departure from the amateur game for Salford Rugby League club.

Championship Table 1966–67

	P	W	D	L	PF	PA	Pts
FRANCE (2)	4	3	0	1	55	41	6
ENGLAND (5)	4	2	0	2	68	67	4
SCOTLAND (2)	4	2	0	2	37	45	4
IRELAND (4)	4	2	0	2	17	22	4
WALES (1)	4	1	0	3	53	55	2

Numbers in brackets indicate last season's positions.

11 November 1967 at Cardiff

WALES 6 (1DG 1PG)
NEW ZEALAND 13 (2G 1PG)

Injuries prevented both Gerald Davies and wonder-boy Keith Jarrett from lining up against Brian Lochore's All Blacks, while after winning 34 caps Swansea's North Welshman Dewi Bebb had retired. Also missing from the Welsh team was David Watkins, whose departure for Salford Rugby League club brought Barry John and Gareth Edwards (both now of Cardiff RFC) together for a first International match as a pair. Wales were manifestly rebuilding, but new skipper Norman Gale still felt that his team would give a good account of itself in what was bound to be a desperately hard encounter.

GARETH EDWARDS: My first recollection from the game is the ashen face of referee Mike Titcomb as props Denzil Williams and Brian Thomas smashed into conflict with Ken Gray and Jaz Muller at the first scrummage. Even in his native West Country, where Gloucestershire and Cornwall traditionally put hard forwards onto the field, I doubt if he had ever seen anything quite as terrifying!

Playing with the elements, New Zealand soon took the lead when full-back Fergie McCormick placed a penalty goal. Minutes later the All Blacks broke up a scrummage wheel by their opponents and spun the ball along the line for centre Bill Davies to beat new cap Ian Hall and send Bill Birtwhistle in at the flag.

GARETH EDWARDS: McCormick's conversion with a wet ball was a superb effort. In those low-scoring days an extra two points meant a lot.

As the visitors turned to face the wind and rain many people doubted that their 8–0 lead would be enough, and sure enough the red forwards provided sufficient possession for Edwards and John to keep play in their opponent's territory. After eight minutes a mighty roar greeted the latter's first score for his country, a dropped goal from just left of the posts.

But five minutes later, against the odds, New Zealand struck again. A speculative penalty attempt by McCormick fell beneath the Welsh posts into the hands of new number 8 forward John Jeffrey. Under pressure, however, the nineteen-year-old sent a rash pass behind him, on to which All Black centre Bill Davis pounced to score. McCormick's conversion put his side ten points up.

BARRY JOHN: As a general rule, failed penalty attempts dropping beneath the crossbar are dealt with by the stand-off half. But in mitigation of poor John Jeffrey's disastrous error, it should be conceded that this shot at goal by McCormick was hanging on the wind and the New Zealand midfield men were following up for all they were worth — so I believe that John was trying to protect me from getting ball and man at once. Whatever the motive, however, our opponents were able to seize a 13–3 lead that made the game safe. At 3–8 down, with the wind, we might just have overhauled them.

Wales kept pounding away at the tourists' defence, pressurizing them into errors which should have yielded penalty points. But the Barry John place-kicking era had yet to open, and Paul Wheeler and Gareth Edwards were both off-target more than once. Nor could Stuart Watkins get the ball to ground after forcing himself across the All Black line. It was in despair that, ten minutes from time, skipper Norman Gale took a penalty which he put

Barry John: an important lesson in tactical kicking.

over with ease for what turned out to be the game's final score.

The Welsh selectors, people say, found themselves unable to forgive poor Jeffrey for his indiscretion. He was never picked for Wales again.

BARRY JOHN: In this match I learned something important about tactical kicking from my opposite number Earle Kirton — namely, that a stand-off half must get as far forward as possible before chipping the ball behind the opposing backs. This allows his centres to pursue the kick at full speed. If he hangs back so must they, to avoid getting offside, and the attack never gains momentum.

MATCH 7

20 January 1968 at Twickenham

ENGLAND 11 (1G 1T 1PG)
WALES 11 (1G 1T 1DG)

FACT BOX

Gareth Edwards became only the second
Welsh scrum half to score since the War –
D. O. Brace having been the first.
For the fourth time in succession England
failed to beat Wales at Twickenham.

England R. B. Hiller, D. H. Prout,
C. W. McFadyean (Captain), R. H. Lloyd,
K. F. Savage, J. F. Finlan, B. W. Redwood,
B. Keen, J. V. Pullin, M. J. Coulman,
M. J. Parsons, P. J. Larter, P. J. Bell, D. J. Gay,
B. R. West.

Wales P. J. Wheeler (Aberavon),
S. J. Watkins (Newport), K. S. Jarrett
(Newport), T. G. R. Davies (Cardiff),
W. K. Jones (Cardiff), B. John (Cardiff),
G. O. Edwards (Cardiff), D. Williams (Ebbw
Vale), N. R. Gale (Llanelli, Captain), R. James
(Bridgend), M. L. Wiltshire (Aberavon),
W. T. Mainwaring (Aberavon), W. D. Morris
(Neath), R. Wanbon (Aberavon), A. J. Gray
(L. Welsh).

SCORERS
England *Tries* – McFadyean, Redwood;
Con. – Hiller; *Pen.* – Hiller.
Wales *Tries* – Edwards, Wanbon;
Con. – Jarrett; *D.G.* – John.

Referee: D. P. d'Arcy (IRFU).

An official newcomer to the Twickenham committee box this day was the former Wales number 8
forward David Nash, whose playing career was
ended prematurely by a severe neck injury suffered
on tour in South Africa with the 1962 British Lions.
His appointment as coach to the National XV was
the first fruit of protracted discussions between top
Welsh administrators about improving the game.
Ex officio, the Ebbw Vale man had sat in on a
selection panel which made five changes from the
team defeated by New Zealand.

GERALD DAVIES: The Welsh Rugby Union itself was
divided over the Nash appointment, which also met with
coolness from senior players like Norman Gale, Brian
Thomas and Alun Pask. Hence, the new coach had to
tread very carefully. Younger team members, including
myself, welcomed his arrival on the scene. At least now we
had direction and continuity, whereas previously there
had been none.

Nash must have been cheered by a sturdy Welsh
performance. At one stage Gale's men trailed by
eight points, before pulling themselves together and
earning a draw.

England's first try came after seven minutes when
Lloyd chipped across the Welsh line for his captain,
Colin McFadyean, to beat a hesitant defence for the
touch-down. The same player, however, soon
knocked on as a Jarrett penalty attempt fell short. At
the five-yard scrummage Gareth Edwards gave
notice of how lethal he was to become from short
range in succeeding years, spotting a blind-side gap
and bursting strongly over for a first International
try.

GARETH EDWARDS: Our hooker Norman Gale had
been taking a hammering at the set scrums from John
Pullin. But he managed to strike perfectly at this one, and
as the ball came sweetly back I *knew* I could score: a
half-dummy, a bit of determination to break a tackle, and
a swallow dive to put the ball down — a gorgeous feeling, I
can tell you!

After this, it was back to defence. The following day a
newspaper carried a graph showing that although each side
got three scores, Wales created only five chances while
England had twenty.

Our opponents' dominance was mainly at the lines-out
where we had no one tall enough to compete with Larter,
Gay and West. These three used a new dodge, the
abbreviated line-out, to tremendous effect.

Before half-time Bob Hiller converted a try by the
Bristol prop Redwood, and soon afterwards
advanced England's lead to 11–3. Then, however,
he was guilty of a bad error, knocking on another
failed Jarrett penalty kick and conceding a five-yard
scrummage from which Bobby Wanbon forced his
way across for a try Jarrett converted.

Still England seemed broadly in control, and it
seemed unlikely that their defence would be pierced
again. Suddenly, however, the speedy London
Welsh flanker Tony Gray caused John Finlan to
miscue a clearance kick, and when Wales won rare
possession from the resultant line-out Barry John
decided that the posts were within range. He let fly
with a drop kick, the low shot cleared the bar, and
Wales were back on terms.

Neither side was able to force the issue in the 25
minutes which remained. This made it eight years

**'As the ball came sweetly back I *knew* I could score' –
Gareth Edwards on his way to a first try for Wales.**

since England had last won this fixture at 'HQ', and
six more were to pass before they could repeat their
victory of 1960.

GARETH EDWARDS: Our new coach David Nash
almost put his foot in it after the game when he told
Wanbon that he should not have scored. He was trying to
make the point that Bobby had not been paying enough
attention to his primary job of shoving at the set
scrummage. But, heck, he'd got three points for us!

I reflected privately that no coach would ever persuade
me to hold my natural instincts in check.

In 1968 the so-called Australian Dispensation rule
was adopted as an experiment. It dispensed with
kicking to touch on the full between the 25-lines,
decreeing that the ball must bounce first, and led
immediately to a more fluent, running type of
rugby. Subsequently, it became a law of the game.

J. P. R. WILLIAMS: Although still a schoolboy at this
time, I welcomed the experiment. It made kicking for
touch a harder option for full-backs, and encouraged them
to counter-attack by running with the ball — which was
the kind of thing I loved.

I was put into the full-back position by my Bridgend
school coach Illtyd Williams. Both he and Sid Hill, the
Millfield School rugby master, favoured adventurous
play, and had consistently advised me to run the ball
upfield and link with the three-quarters whenever I saw an
opportunity.

31

3 February 1968 at Cardiff

WALES   5 (1G)
SCOTLAND   0

FACT BOX

This was Wales's only victory of the 1967–68 season.

Wales D. Rees (Swansea), S. J. Watkins (Newport), K. S. Jarrett (Newport), T. G. R. Davies (Cardiff), W. K. Jones (Cardiff), B. John (Cardiff), G. O. Edwards (Cardiff, Captain), D. J. Lloyd (Bridgend), J. Young (Bridgend), J. P. O'Shea (Cardiff), M. L. Wiltshire (Aberavon), W. D. Thomas (Llanelli), W. D. Morris (Neath), R. E. Jones (Coventry), A. J. Gray (L. Welsh).
Scotland S. Wilson, G. J. Keith, J. N. M. Frame, J. W. C. Turner, A. J. W. Hinshelwood, D. H. Chisholm, A. J. Hastie, A. B. Carmichael, F. A. L. Laidlaw, D. M. D. Rollo, P. K. Stagg, G. W. E. Mitchell, J. P. Fisher (Captain), A. H. W. Boyle, T. G. Elliot.
SCORERS
Wales *Try* – K. Jones; *Con.* – Jarrett.
Referee: G. C. Lamb (RFU).

Not for the first time, changes in their team made by the Welsh selectors generated more excitement than the match itself. A ruthlessly wielded axe toppled the full-back of Twickenham, Paul Wheeler, and no fewer than five forwards — Norman Gale, Denzil Williams, Bill Mainwaring, 'Boyo' James and Bobby Wanbon. Back came John Lloyd and John O'Shea at prop, Delme Thomas at lock and Ron Jones at number 8, while new caps were awarded to a hooker from Bridgend RFC, Jeff Young, and a full-back from Swansea, diminutive Doug Rees. The last selection signified that despite his sensational debut at full-back for Wales in 1967, Keith Jarrett was now categorized as a centre.

But the most radical move was to give Gareth Edwards the captaincy.

GARETH EDWARDS: Although things had gone well for me in leading East Wales to a draw with the unbeaten All Blacks I know now — with hindsight — that I was not ready for the job. A couple of seasons as vice-captain first would have been better preparation. The truth is that with a number of old stalwarts creaking at the joints, the Welsh selectors were clutching at straws when they made me skipper.

But captaincy in no way inhibited my approach, as some people have suggested. I always felt able to do my own thing when I wanted to.

Looking back, observers sometimes ask themselves why the selectors turned to Edwards rather than his elder, Barry John. The reason perhaps lies in the respective images projected by the two great players. John disguised total inner commitment with a front that often seemed flippant, characterized by an engaging grin. Edwards, his face always a mask except when demanding more effort

from team-mates, appeared the more serious and involved of the pair — a Cromwell rather than a Cavalier. John later admitted in his autobiography, moreover, that he never fancied what he called 'the authority part' of captaincy.

However, Edwards's leadership could not inspire his men to a great performance, and Wales had to be content with the single goal which came 15 minutes into the match. Keith Jarrett broke past his opposite number before releasing what many onlookers — and Scottish players — viewed as a forward pass to Gerald Davies.

GERALD DAVIES: I fed Keri Jones the ball with Scotland's defence in disarray, and his great speed did the rest.

But as for having received a forward pass from Keith — well, after many years that is news to me! I can honestly say the thought never crossed my mind.

Jarrett, whose place kicking this day was otherwise indifferent, put over the conversion. Although the game had little else of note to offer, Scotland were well policed throughout, and seldom looked like registering a second victory at Cardiff in forty years.

In retrospect the Welsh team of the day can be seen to have contained the nucleus of the great sides of the 'seventies. Gerald Davies, Barry John and Gareth Edwards had by now done enough to be established behind the scrum, while Delme Thomas, Dai Morris, Jeff Young and John Lloyd were forwards who had many caps to look forward to.

33

9 March 1968 in Dublin
IRELAND 9 (1T 1DG 1PG)
WALES 6 (1DG 1PG)

FACT BOX

A remarkably junior-looking XV represented Wales this day – with just 55 caps between them (compared with 190 in the opposition ranks).

Ireland T. J. Kiernan (Captain), A. T. A. Duggan, L Hunter, F. P. K. Bresnihan, J. C. M. Moroney, G. M. H. Gibson, R. M. Young, P. O'Callaghan, A. M. Brady, S. Millar, W. J. McBride, M. G. Molloy, M. G. Doyle, K. G. Goodall, T. J. Doyle.

Wales D. Rees (Swansea), W. K. Jones (Cardiff), S. J. Dawes (L. Welsh, Captain), W. H. Raybould (L. Welsh), M. C. R. Richards (Cardiff), B. John (Cardiff), G. O. Edwards (Cardiff), J. P. O'Shea (Cardiff), J. Young (Bridgend), D. J. Lloyd (Bridgend), I. C. Jones (L. Welsh), W. D. Thomas (Llanelli), W. D. Morris (Neath), R. E. Jones (Coventry), J. Taylor (L. Welsh).

SCORERS
Ireland *Try* – Mick Doyle; *Pen.* – Kiernan; *D.G.* – Gibson.
Wales *Pen.* – Rees; *D.G.* – Edwards.

Referee: M. H. Titcomb (RFU).

BARRY JOHN: Great people, the Irish, and wonderful company. But on a rugby field they come at you like bats out of hell!

The fame of Welsh starlets Barry John and Gareth Edwards had gone ahead of them, drawing a capacity crowd to watch their Lansdowne Road debuts. But the Welsh team bore only a faint resemblance to that which had beaten Scotland. The rise to pre-eminence of London Welsh RFC was acknowledged by the awarding of further caps to John Taylor and Billy Raybould, as well as a first one to Ian Jones. Further, club skipper John Dawes took over his country's captaincy from Gareth Edwards.

PHIL BENNETT: As a reserve, I heard John's pre-match pep-talk in which he urged the boys to throw the ball about in London Welsh fashion, running from all sorts of positions and counter-attacking whenever possible. Alas, this was International rugby and the Irish tacklers knocked our players down hard and ruthlessly.

There are two teams in any game, and the opposition is always keyed up to prevent your side playing the way it wants to.

This was not a match to be remembered for flashes of genius from the young Welshmen, or any novelty from a home side under the rock-like Tom Kiernan. Rather was it genial Englishman Mike Titcomb who disitnguished himself with a refereeing decision that enraged the Irish rugby fraternity.

In the first half the tearaway men in green went ahead through a Kiernan penalty and a Mike Gibson dropped goal. John Taylor led a sortie to Ireland's 25-line, where a penalty for foot up at the scrummage was kicked by Welsh full-back Doug Rees.

The Irish, turning to face the breeze at the break, thus faced a long haul, and sure enough the visitors were soon camped on their 25-line. Here, at a line-

Tall Irish number eight forward Ken Goodall was always a thorn in the Welsh flesh. Here his victim is Maurice Richards.

out on the Welsh left, Delme Thomas delivered precise possession to Gareth Edwards, who instantly dropped for goal. The ball soared towards the Irish posts.

A skirmish of skippers. . . . Although half beaten Tom Kiernan has just enough hold on John Dawes to force the Welshman to look for support.

GARETH EDWARDS: It left my foot beautifully, and instinctively as it began travelling straight and true I exclaimed 'Yes!' Referee Titcomb, who had been watching the Irish back row men for possible offside, turned just too late to see the ball's last-minute swing outside one of the posts, and awarded the score.

It was an understandable mistake and a genuine one — can you imagine an Englishman, of all people, giving Wales something for nothing! We got a lucky three points, agreed — but there've been other days when the luck has gone against us. These things even out over the years.

All hullabaloo broke out on the terraces. During a three-minute delay the ball was detained by the crowd while bottles, tin cans, fruit and even spectators sailed on to the pitch in its place. The referee

had to endure a further thirty-seven minutes of booing and abuse with the game apparently stuck at stalemate. But providentially for him, an injury-time attack launched by Mike Gibson swept play to the Welsh corner flag, where after a furious mêlée Mick Doyle managed to cross for an unconverted try. The wags say Mr Titcomb blew for time from the dressing-room!

BARRY JOHN: I hold just one thing against my Irish friends — I was never on a winning side in Dublin!

Things might have been different in 1968 — and 1970 — if Wales could have got a lead. Perhaps then Ireland might have folded. But we always seemed to be playing from behind at Lansdowne Road.

35

23 March 1968 at Cardiff

WALES 9 (1T 2PG)
FRANCE 14 (1G 1T 1PG)

FACT BOX

Wales's defeat was to be their last Championship reverse at Cardiff until Scotland's victory there in 1982.

Wales D. Rees (Swansea), W. K. Jones (Cardiff), S. J. Dawes (L. Welsh), W. H. Raybould (L. Welsh), M. C. R. Richards (Cardiff), B. John (Cardiff), G. O. Edwards (Cardiff, Captain), D. J. Lloyd (Bridgend), J. Young (Bridgend), J. P. O'Shea (Cardiff), W. D. Thomas (Llanelli), M. L. Wiltshire (Aberavon), W. D. Morris (Neath), R. E. Jones (Coventry), J. Taylor (L. Welsh).

France C. Lacazè, J-M. Bonal, J. Maso, C. Dourthe, A. Campaes, G. Camberabero, L. Camberabero, J-C. Noble, M. Yachvili, M. Lasserre, A. Plantefol, E. Cester, W. Spanghero, M. Greffe, C. Carrere (Captain).

SCORERS
Wales *Try* – Keri Jones; *Pens.* – Rees (2).
France *Tries* – L. Camberabero, Carrere; *Con.* – G. Camberabero; *Pen.* – G. Camberabero; *D.G.* – G. Camberabero.

Referee: H. B. Laidlaw (SRU).

Wales hooker Jeff Young protects hard-won possession at a line-out. But France were not to be denied their red-letter day.

A red-letter day at Cardiff Arms Park: for the first time since entering the Championship in 1910, France completed a Grand Slam. British fans took off their hats to the Tricolours.

The Welsh had made one team change, reintroducing Max Wiltshire at lock in place of Ian Jones, while Gareth Edwards had been given back the captaincy.

GARETH EDWARDS: Neither losing the captaincy for the Irish match nor getting it back again for this one had much effect on my personal feelings. It said more about the selectors than about me. They just couldn't make up their minds.

When the skipper and his team awoke on a wet and wind-swept Saturday morning they must have felt that the gods had delivered opponents from the Mediterranean coast's hard, sun-baked grounds straight into their hands. And initially they gave their supporters something to shout about, sweeping to a six-point lead through a Doug Rees penalty goal and a smart try by Keri Jones. Guy Camberabero dropped a smart goal, but another penalty by their full-back saw Wales reach the interval 9–3 ahead.

Walter Spanghero of Narbonne, however, now turned in what was described as the finest forty minutes' rugby of his career, revitalizing a French pack which seemed to have given up the ghost. Swarming all over a disconcerted Welsh defence, the magnificent eight soon set up a try for their captain Carrere.

GARETH EDWARDS: The French back row of this era — Spanghero, Carrere and Dauga or Salut — were tremendously creative, always trying to develop moves between each other. Their preoccupation with attack sometimes meant that an opposing scrum-half got a little extra latitude.

But, as in this game, it also meant endless tackling in support of one's own forwards as the French surged around scrummages or peeled off the end of the line-out.

Fortunately, I enjoyed tackling. There was always a great thrill in pitting my body strength against someone else's, and knowing that my frame could take the bumps.

With Wales still reeling, Lilian Camberabero scorched around the blind side for a try which took France into the lead. A conversion and penalty by his brother lifted the family contribution to 11 of the winners' 14 points.

So the Welsh had to settle for fourth place in the Five Nations Championship, with France on top for the second year in succession.

GARETH EDWARDS: Having criticized the selectors for inconsistency over the captaincy I must now concede that in one respect they showed great faith in some of us newer players.

Barry John, for instance, had now played seven times for Wales and been on a winning side just once. I had six caps but had taken part in only two victories. Not an altogether auspicious start for either of us!

Championship Table 1967–68

	P	W	D	L	PF	PA	Pts
FRANCE (1)	4	4	0	0	52	30	8
IRELAND (2)	4	2	1	1	38	37	5
ENGLAND (2)	4	1	2	1	37	40	4
WALES (5)	4	1	1	2	31	34	3
SCOTLAND (2)	4	0	0	4	18	35	0

Numbers in brackets indicate last season's positions.

1 February 1969 at Murrayfield
SCOTLAND 3 (1PG)
WALES 17 (1G 2T 2PG)

Enter two more of the giants: a cold Edinburgh afternoon and debuts for Wales by Mervyn Davies at number 8 and John Williams at full-back, both members of London Welsh RFC. 'JPR', as he came to be known, had been an outstanding schoolboy player, had gained experience with Bridgend RFC, and was now a medical student in London.

J. P. R. WILLIAMS: I had been blooded in Argentina the previous summer when a Welsh side, without its British Lions, drew one unofficial Test and lost the other. The South Americans christened me 'Canasta' — Basket — because I gathered high kicks safely.

New Wales team coach Clive Rowlands . . . pioneering 'squad sessions'.

Although I have always sought to conceal nerves, I certainly had butterflies in Edinburgh. But after breakfast I remember strolling along Princes Street, whose whole length was crammed with supporters in red and white, all wanting to shake my hand and wish me well. Terrific!

Merv the Swerve had come up the hard way, despite being the son of a Victory International player. Penlan School in Swansea did not enjoy the fashionable reputation for rugby of other Welsh schools, so Davies cut little ice with influential onlookers until he gained a teaching post in London and joined London Welsh.

MERVYN DAVIES: At Old Deer Park I established myself as someone who could provide possession from lines-out and mauls. I won an International Trial and when the senior number 8 forward Dennis Hughes damaged an achilles tendon I was promoted to the Reds, doing well enough to be picked for the Murrayfield match.

The two recruits joined a confident Welsh side, to captain which Brian Price of Newport RFC had been recalled after a year's absence from representative rugby. Heavy rain stopped falling just before the game began, and although the visitors had to play into the wind, Jarrett's form with the boot was good, and he punished Scotland with penalty goals for offside and foot up.

J. P. R. WILLIAMS: Early in the game I collected a Scottish kick-ahead with some space to work in. Barry John called 'Move it!' and we brought off a scissors ploy. That helped me to settle down.

MERVYN DAVIES: Mindful of fatal errors made by predecessors like John Jeffrey, I simply concentrated grimly on eliminating mistakes from my play. So my main recollections of the game concern Scotland's number 8 Jim Telfer, and the number of times he lay on the ball and prevented us from winning it!

I found the new standard faster and tougher than club rugby but I can honestly say I found little difficulty adjusting to it.

Observers considered that the Welsh pack was particularly well knit together. The reason doubtless lay in the 'squad sessions' being pioneered by the new team coach, former International scrum half Clive Rowlands. Some minutes into the second half the Scots were violently wheeled near their own goal-line, and as McCrae fumbled his pass to Colin Telfer, Gareth Edwards swept around to rob him and cross for a neat try.

Wing Maurice Richards was soon the recipient of a line-out tap from Brian Price, and scored Wales's second try. Full-back Blaikie kicked Scotland's solitary penalty goal, before Barry John set the seal on a great triumph for the visitors. Charging down a Telfer clearance, he was agile enough to pick up the loose ball at full speed. Regaining balance, he out-paced Blaikie and crossed at the posts for a first International try. The conversion was a formality for Jarrett, and Wales had made their best start to a Championship campaign since 1966.

A second try for Wales: Maurice Richards the scorer.

MATCH 12

8 March 1969 at Cardiff

WALES 24 (3G 1T 1DG 1PG)
IRELAND 11 (1G 2PG)

Outrage written all over the profile of Wales skipper Brian Price *(centre, left)* and Ireland's Noel Murphy *(centre, right)* reels under a knock-out punch. Although provoked, Price was fortunate to escape with a warning for taking the law into his own fists.

FACT BOX

In 1968 the Welsh Rugby Union embarked upon the re-building of the National Ground at Cardiff Arms Park. As a first stage the North Stand had been demolished, so that attendance was limited to 29,000 — roughly half of the arena's previous capacity. Consistent wing Stuart Watkins scored his ninth, and last, International try.

Wales J. P. R. Williams (L. Welsh), S. J. Watkins (Newport), K. S. Jarrett (Newport), T. G. R. Davies (Cardiff), M. C. R. Richards (Cardiff), B. John (Cardiff), G. O. Edwards (Cardiff), D. Williams (Ebbw Vale), J. Young (Bridgend), D. J. Lloyd (Bridgend), B. Price (Newport, Captain), B. Thomas (Neath), W. D. Morris (Neath), T. M. Davies (L. Welsh), J. Taylor (L. Welsh).

Ireland T. J. Kiernan (Captain), A. T. A. Duggan, F. P. K. Bresnihan, C. M. H. Gibson, J. C. M. Moroney, B. J. McGann, R. M. Young, P. O'Callaghan, K. W. Kennedy, S. Millar, W. J. McBride, M. G. Molloy, J. C. Davidson, M. L. Hipwell, N. A. Murphy.

SCORERS
Wales *Tries* – Watkins, Morris, Taylor, Denzil Williams; *Cons.* – Jarrett (3); *Pen.* – Jarrett; *D.G.* – John.
Ireland *Try* – Gibson; *Con.* – Kiernan; *Pens,* – Kiernan (2).

Referee: D. C. J. McMahon (SRU).

This was a match full of bad blood and temper and impartial critics did not like what they saw. Gordon Ross, editor of the now defunct *Playfair Annual*, wrote that 'irreparable harm' had been done to the game in the eyes of millions of television viewers. The Welsh, who rate the Irish as their most 'physical' opponents, were not as unhappy. Their biggest victory over Ireland since 1907 satisfactorily anaesthetized the sting of three successive defeats at the hands of their Celtic cousins.

The match began sensationally. Within three minutes of courteously introducing his team to the Prince of Wales, Brian Price had floored Irish flanker Noel Murphy with a punch that would have guaranteed him ABA honours at Wembley. Most onlookers guessed that the Welsh captain had been provoked, but they also thought him lucky not be sent off by Scots referee D. C. J. McMahon. Later in the first half, hooker Ken Kennedy became another victim of rough Welsh justice, but the match finished with thirty players still afield.

GARETH EDWARDS: Looking back, I can chuckle at what took place, but it was pretty frightening at the time!

Our players rated Noel Murphy highly on the previous summer's Lions tour, and we had a plan to blunt his keenness for the action. It was perfectly legitimate, and simply involved rucking him in New Zealand style as early as possible in the game. However, a spy leaked this

'Murphy Plan' (though not its details) to the Irish camp; so as soon as Brian hit Noel, Tom Kiernan came protesting from full back, 'Hey, ref! It's the bloody Murphy Plan! Send Price off!'

For half an hour the Irish were absolutely bananas! I was terrified to go down on the ball in case one of them exacted revenge. Phil O'Callaghan, for instance, was frightening just to look at. With his steely eyes and bristling crew-cut he reminded you of a villain out of a James Bond film.

When Kennedy claimed to have been punched too, that was nearly the last straw. Tom Kiernan threatened to take his team off the field. He didn't forgive Wales for two or three seasons.

Kiernan it was, however, who kicked Ireland into the lead with a penalty goal, repeating his success after Barry John had dropped a goal for Wales. Quick thinking by the home team next earned them the lead after they had won a penalty on their opponents' 25-line. Mindful of Keith Jarrett's goal-kicking capability, the Irish withdrew to their line, but the Newport man made no signal to Mr McMahon that he would kick at the posts. Instead he nudged the ball to the unmarked Denzil Williams, who trundled in for a soft try. Jarrett put the conversion over.

After the interval Ireland fell apart, with Barry John first to cause confusion in their ranks. Accelerating around the opposing back row, he tossed a high pass to Stuart Watkins which the wing did well to catch and touch down for a second try. Then it was Gareth Edwards's turn to set up a score, converted by Jarrett, for close-supporting flanker Dai Morris — not for nothing would he come to be known as 'the Shadow'.

GARETH EDWARDS: Dai was an unsung hero, but a joy for a scrum-half to work with. So often, when I broke, he was correctly placed for a pass.

John Taylor, beginning to perfect the open-side support play for which he too was to become celebrated, now rounded off spectacular passing by the backs with a swallow dive to score at the corner. After Jarrett had converted with a superb kick the Welsh eased their foot from the throttle and allowed Mike Gibson to win a thrilling race after a loose ball for a try which Kiernan converted. Jarrett put over a final penalty goal, and Ireland left for home empty-handed.

MATCH 13

22 March 1969 at Stade Colombes
FRANCE 8 (1G 1PG)
WALES 8 (1G 1T)

FACT BOX

Three contributors won their tenth caps —
Barry John, Gareth Edwards and Gerald
Davies.
Lock forward and skipper Brian Price was
paying his fifth (and final) visit to Colombes —
where he was never on a winning side. On this
day, however, Wales broke a dismal sequence
of five defeats in Paris to earn their first-ever
draw there.

France P. Villepreux, B. Moraitis, C. Dourthe,
J. Trillo, A. Campaes, J. Maso, G. Sutra,
J. Iracabal, R. Benesis, J-L. Azarete,
A. Plantefol, E. Cester, P. Biemouret,
W. Spanghero (Captain), G. Viard.

Wales J. P. R. Williams (L. Welsh),
S. J. Watkins (Newport), K. S. Jarrett
(Newport), T. G. R. Davies (Cardiff),
M. C. R. Richards (Cardiff), B. John (Cardiff),
G. O. Edwards (Cardiff), D. Williams (Ebbw
Vale), J. Young, (Bridgend), D. J. Lloyd
(Bridgend), B. Price (Newport, Captain),
B. Thomas (Neath), W. D. Morris (Neath),
T. M. Davies (L. Welsh), J. Taylor (L. Welsh).
Replacement: P. Bennett (Llanelli) for
Gerald Davies.

SCORERS
France *Try* – Campaes; *Con.* – Villepreux;
Pen. – Villepreux.
Wales *Tries* – Edwards, Richards;
Con. – Jarrett.

Referee: R. F. Burrell (SRU).

Phil Bennett failed to touch the ball in this game, but
still went into the archives of rugby football as
Wales's first International replacement. The young
stand-off half from Llanelli RFC took over from
Gerald Davies shortly before no-side when the
centre dislocated an elbow.

PHIL BENNETT: The medical officer finished examin-
ing Gerald and nodded permission for me to go on, but —
horror of horrors! — I couldn't get my track suit off.
Norman Gale had to rip the zip-fasteners away from my
ankles.

When I finally came out of the tunnel the frenzy and
hysteria absolutely terrified me. Barry John took one look
at this shivering replacement and decided there was no
way he dared pass the ball! He plugged the touch-line in
the couple of minutes that were left.

Wales had arrived in Paris with high hopes, and, for
the third successive fixture, an unchanged XV. And
had it been the fashion to make individual awards in
those days Gareth Edwards would surely have been
named man of the match. After 25 minutes Jarrett
burst down the French left, finding ready support
from John Taylor; Edwards was the recipient of the
flanker's quick pass, and elected to keep going
despite the proximity of four French defenders.

GARETH EDWARDS: A side-step saw one of them off,
and the next two seemed to get in each other's way,
pushing and pulling me onwards. In the end it was just a
matter of forcing myself to earth across the line, with the
last Frenchman trying vainly to hold me up.

People say it was one of my better tries. I like to think
that it owed much to the gymnastic ability of which I was
very proud at school.

Certainly this was a score that very few scrum-halves
in history could have obtained. Jarrett hit an upright
with his conversion attempt, but before half-time
Edwards had set up another try which brought
warm applause from the Colombes crowd. Racing
on to a chip by the scrum-half which bounced
awkwardly for the French defenders, Maurice
Richards crossed at the corner flag.

GARETH EDWARDS: The responsibility for the timing
of this move lies with the wing, and all credit to Maurice
for getting it right.

Jarrett put over what turned out to be an important
conversion, but though they needed only one score
to make the match safe, the visitors' great effort now
faded as Pierre Villepreux opened France's account
with a 45-yard penalty goal. Soon afterwards the
full-back put up a high ball which had the Welsh
defenders back-pedalling desperately towards their
goal-line. It was André Campaes, however, who
sprinted through to seize possession and score at the
posts. Villepreux converted, and the scores were
level.

The pendulum had swung decisively in favour of
the home side, whose supporters roared them on
while Wales battled doggedly for the draw.
Colombes had proved too great a hurdle for a Welsh
team and its Grand Slam ambitions.

PHIL BENNETT: After the game I felt a bit sheepish, since I had spent only a minute or two on the field and hadn't got into the action.

But then Dennis Hughes of Newbridge said to me, 'Whatever happens now, Phil, they can't take that away from you. You're a Welsh International.' That made my day.

Edwards the competitor: 'In the end it was just a matter of forcing myself to earth across the line.'

43

12 April 1969 at Cardiff

WALES 30 (3G 2T 1DG 2PG)
ENGLAND 9 (3PG)

Despite the absence through injury of skipper Brian Price and Gerald Davies, Wales battered England to defeat by the biggest margin since 1922. Their Five Nations' title and Triple Crown signalled the beginning of a dominance in Europe that was to last broadly for a decade. Moreover, the manner of victory in this match — imaginative, clean, entertaining — erased uncomfortable memories of the disagreeable encounter with Ireland. The day's personal triumph belonged to Cardiff wing Maurice Richards, whose four tries equalled a long-standing record held jointly by Willie Llewellyn and Reggie Gibbs.

GERALD DAVIES: Maurice was a terrific player. In his early days as a centre he tried to do too much himself, so the move to wing was a good thing.

He had all the skills: speed off the mark, a body swerve, a gigantic side-step and a powerful hand-off. He also hated to stay tackled, so that unless an opponent gripped him like a vice Maurice would bob up like a jack-in-the-box and carry on running.

There were long faces around the gaunt, half-finished stadium when Bob Hiller's down-wind penalty gave England the lead. But a clever build-up in which Stuart Watkins and Barry John were prominent led to Maurice Richards's first try and a 3–3 interval score.

Then the Welsh cut loose, encouraged by two penalties kicked by Jarrett and his conversion of a superb try by Barry John which left a trail of Englishmen sprawling in his wake. At last the stand-off had brought to his International play the swerving, effortless running with which he demoralized opponents of Cardiff.

BARRY JOHN: This game was a watershed for me. Suddenly I had had enough of doing what other people said, deciding to be the puppet-master, not a puppet.

Keith Jarrett set up my try, with one of those tantalizing glimpses of his potential that he gave before turning professional. A nice little 'nine-iron' by him bounced perfectly for me, tracking along in my customary sweeper role just behind the centres. When I gathered the ball England's tacklers were on the wrong foot, and the try was waiting to be scored.

The remaining twenty-six minutes still held top-notch entertainment for an enthralled crowd. Maybe Richards's three further tries owed much to marvellous play by those inside him; nevertheless, wings do drop the ball occasionally, so he won high acclaim for his accurate and devastating finishing. Barry John dropped a goal — the only one he kicked for Wales with the left foot — Jarrett's two final conversions gave him a 31-point total for the Championship season, while Bob Hiller was applauded for completing a hat-trick of penalty goals.

It had been a fine campaign for Wales. Sound selection was supported by the inspired coaching of Clive Rowlands, who had ignited in his men what Aneurin Bevan used to call 'fire in the belly'. Individual newcomers had also come good: Mervyn Davies and Jeff Young were junior members of a pack that had shown skill and control without losing its desire to dominate; while John Williams had brought a sense of security to the full-back position which encouraged his team-mates to experiment with their whole bag of tricks.

J. P. R. WILLIAMS: As a student at St Mary's Hospital I had a special reason for wanting to finish on the winning side against England. Had we lost, the amount of leg-pulling I would have had to suffer on my return to London would have been intolerable!

Championship Table 1968–69

	P	W	D	L	PF	PA	Pts
WALES (4)	4	3	1	0	79	31	7
IRELAND (2)	4	3	0	1	61	48	6
ENGLAND (3)	4	2	0	2	54	58	4
SCOTLAND (5)	4	1	0	3	12	44	2
FRANCE (1)	4	0	1	3	28	53	1

Maurice Richards . . . equalling a record that had stood for 70 years. 'Maurice had all the skills,' says Gerald Davies.

Numbers in brackets indicate last season's positions.

31 May 1969 at Christchurch
NEW ZEALAND 19 (2G 2T 1PG)
WALES 0

FACT BOX

New Zealand W. F. McCormick, M. J. Dick, W. L. Davis, G. S. Thorne, I. R. McRae, E. W. Kirton, S. M. Going, K. F. Gray, B. E. McLeod, B. L. Muller, C. E. Meads, A. E. Smith, T. N. Lister, B. J. Lochore (Captain), I. A. Kirkpatrick.

Wales J. P. R. Williams (L. Welsh), M. C. R. Richards (Cardiff), T. G. R. Davies (Cardiff), K. S. Jarrett (Newport), S. J. Watkins (Newport), B. John (Cardiff), G. O. Edwards (Cardiff), D. Williams (Ebbw Vale), J. Young (Bridgend), D. J. Lloyd (Bridgend), B. Price (Newport, Captain), B. Thomas (Neath), W. D. Morris (Neath), T. M. Davies (L. Welsh), J. Taylor (L. Welsh). *Replacement:* N. R. Gale (Llanelli) for Jeff Young.

SCORERS
New Zealand *Tries* – Dick, McLeod, Lochore, Gray; *Cons.* – McCormick (2); *Pen.* – McCormick.

Referee: P. Murphy (N. Auckland).

This was a Test Match which New Zealand had been waiting to win ever since Wales robbed the First All Blacks of an unbeaten 1905 tour record with a controversial 3–0 victory in Cardiff. Looking back on it, however, many onlookers believe that an imbalance of skill was not the main factor to blame for the visitors' heavy reverse at Christchurch.

BARRY JOHN: They are quite right — much blame must rest on the WRU administrators of the day, 12,000 miles away in Cardiff, who had no idea at all of the impossible commitment they had let us in for.

We had to play this vital match just six days after flying non-stop from London to Auckland. To underline how travel-weary the Welsh party was, let me quote just two examples: an earthquake shook New Plymouth the night before we played Taranaki, but not one of our boys was woken by it.

After fourteen victories in succession, dating back to 1965, New Zealand were able to field a settled, confident XV for the Lancaster Park clash. Many home supporters thought it the best side in All Black history, and it certainly carried too many guns for the Welsh. After fifteen minutes Colin Meads won line-out possession near half-way, and Graham Thorne was put menacingly away down a wing. The ball came back via Bruce McLeod and Earle Kirton to Malcolm Dick, who scored an unconverted try at the corner. Already it was noticeable that the home pack were seizing the whip-hand.

MERVYN DAVIES: The All Black forwards were everything we were not — more massively built, better coordinated, better handlers and above all faster and more effective on the lose ball.

Before long prop Brian Muller profited from a mistake by Stuart Watkins to send McLeod hurtling 20 yards to the posts for a try converted by full-back Fergie McCormick, who was again successful after Brian Lochore had become New Zealand's third try-scorer.

BARRY JOHN: Our opponents' finishing was tremendous. Nevertheless, we did create some scoring chances. I managed to put a couple of grub kicks behind the All Black centres, but on both occasions the bounce was unkind to Maurice Richards on the wing.

The tourists were now forced to close ranks and defend doggedly. But ten minutes from no-side Thorne again beat his marker and linked with the New Zealand forwards. Ken Gray was the final handler in a tremendous foray which swept all before it and ended in an unconverted try. McCormick rounded off the All Blacks' day with a 35-yard penalty goal.

Shortly before the end, as the home pack roared away from a line-out, Wales's hooker Jeff Young was felled, and left the field with a cracked jaw-bone. The referee singled out Meads for a severe warning, and the big lock later explained that Young had been dealt unofficial justice for persistent jersey-tugging. However, the injury to their hooker was but one of many wounds the visitors were left to lick.

MERVYN DAVIES: The blow to our pride was all the more hurtful since we had arrived in New Zealand thinking we were the greatest. We agreed that there was only one word to describe what had happened to us — annihilation.

Gerald Davies: after this huge defeat his future for Wales lay on the wing.

MATCH 16

14 June 1969 at Auckland

NEW ZEALAND 33 (3G 1DG 5PG)
WALES 12 (2T 2PG)

FACT BOX

Fergie McCormick set a new world record for points scored in an International match by an individual. His 24 points surpassed the 22 by D. Mare (South Africa v. France, 1907) and D. Lambert (England v. France, 1911).
New Zealand's 33 points were their highest against Wales, 21 their biggest winning margin.
For Wales this was the biggest defeat since 1924 and Scotland's 35—10 victory.

New Zealand   W. F. McCormick, M. J. Dick, W. L. Davis, G. R. Skudder, I. R. McRae, E. W. Kirton, S. M. Going, K. F. Gray, B. E. McLeod, A. E. Hopkinson, C. E. Meads, A. E. Smith, T. N. Lister, B. J. Lochore (Captain), I. A. Kirkpatrick.

Wales   J. P. R. Williams (L. Welsh), M. C. R. Richards (Cardiff), S. J. Dawes (L. Welsh), K. S. Jarrett (Newport), T. G. R. Davies (Cardiff), B. John (Cardiff), G. O. Edwards (Cardiff), D. Williams (Ebbw Vale), N. R. Gale (Llanelli), B. Thomas (Neath), W. D. Thomas (Llanelli), B. Price (Newport, Captain), W. D. Morris (Neath), T. M. Davies (L. Welsh), D. Hughes (Newbridge).

SCORERS
New Zealand   Tries – Skudder, McRae, Kirkpatrick; Cons. – McCormick (3); Pens. – McCormick (5); D.G. – McCormick.
Wales   Tries – Jarrett, Richards; Pens. – Jarrett (2).

Referee: P. Murphy (N. Auckland).

Further acclimatization helped Wales to wins over Otago and Wellington, which sent them into the Second Test greatly encouraged — and much re-organized. John Lloyd and John Taylor lost their places to Brian Thomas and Dennis Hughes, Delme Thomas came into the second row, and after eleven appearances in the midfield Gerald Davies moved to the right wing in place of Stuart Watkins. Never again would the Carmarthenshire man play representative rugby in the centre, whereas his performances in the new position were to bring all kinds of brilliance and dazzle to the world's arenas in the coming decade.

GERALD DAVIES: Clive Rowlands gave me the news on the journey between Wellington and Auckland that I would be on the wing, as all the regulars were on our injury list. I suspect that my team-mates were a bit worried about how I would play, while my own reaction was distinct pique at what I saw as a demotion.

But as the game progressed I put in some running with the ball, helping Wales on one occasion to the position from which Maurice Richards scored, and thought at the end that the experience had not been too disagreeable. Tour colleague Jeff Young said, 'You came out of it all right.' That was encouraging.

No amount of reshuffling availed that day, however, despite a good early showing by the visitors. Jarrett and McCormick exchanged penalty goals before John Williams came up into the line and put Maurice Richards away for an unconverted try to follow the hat-trick he had recorded against Otago.

J. P. R. WILLIAMS: We won the ball at a line-out and my contribution was to come up fast outside the left centre to make an extra man. The All Blacks were occasionally vulnerable to the move, since their wings tended to stray infield to tackle the ball-carrier. That is what happened this time, and I was able to put Maurice away with room to move.

Kirton and McCormick seemed to have him covered, but a side-step and change of pace left them for dead.

The All Blacks hit back with a flourish. Brian Lochore fed Sid Going away from a scrum near the Welsh 25, and George Skudder received the scrum-half's scoring pass. The conversion by McCormick, plus two more penalties, gave the home side a 14–6 interval lead.

New Zealand's full-back was on target again soon afterwards, as was Jarrett, who at last broke a sequence of bad misses. Midway through the half, however, Wales's resistance was finally broken. Going initiated a move carried on by McLeod and Lister, and although the tacklers did not flinch, ultra-close support play by New Zealand finally put MacRae clear to crash in at the posts. On his way to a world record, McCormick put over the conversion before underlining his team's brimming confidence with a 55-yard dropped goal off a loose Welsh clearance. The full-back's final points came from his fifth penalty and the conversion of Ian Kirkpatrick's try.

Keith Jarrett got a second try for Wales in injury time, but the European champions left for Australia with tails tucked firmly between their legs.

New Zealand full back Fergie McCormick: a 24-point
world record.

MERVYN DAVIES: There was a silver lining. I and the
other young players agreed that there was no way we were
ever going to take a hiding like that again. Thus I think the
Welsh approach to rugby in the 'seventies was toughened
and hardened.

BARRY JOHN: Both the All Blacks' mammoth score and
Fergie McCormick's world record owed much to Pat
Murphy's refereeing, about which volumes of harsh words
have been spoken and penned by Welshmen who were in

Auckland on this day. To people who believe that we were
exaggerating and that time heals most wounds, let me say
that Mr Murphy remains the best living argument for
neutral referees I have ever seen.

Some of his decisions against Wales defied explanation
— and drove our players, notably Gareth and myself, to
howl such abuse at him that we must have been sent off by
a man in his right senses. Murphy's whole approach,
however, was so malign that it seemed he was dazed and
drunk from New Zealand's success.

Lest I am accused of sour grapes let me add quickly that
the New Zealand side of 1969 was in a different class from
ourselves. It is probably the best team I ever played
against.

49

MATCH 17

21 June 1969 at Sydney

AUSTRALIA 16 (2G 2PG)
WALES 19 (2G 1T 2PG)

On the flight to Australia tour manager Handel Rogers and coach Clive Rowlands worked flat out to reflate their men's sagging morale. Looking on the bright side, they spoke of a reasonable record outside the Tests in New Zealand, which included the scalp of that most formidable province Otago. And they told the players they could not afford to think the hardest part of the tour was over, since twelve months earlier the Wallabies had lost only 19–18 to the All Blacks. It would not be easy to gain revenge for Australia's 1966 victory in Cardiff.

GERALD DAVIES: But management had a hard job motivating the party. Exhausted after the journey, most players took a dim view of coach Clive Rowlands's plan to train on a municipal pitch soon after disembarking. 'No more press-ups for me!' announced skipper Brian Price!

GARETH EDWARDS: But I for one was dead keen. Having felt a twinge in a hamstring early in the First Test at Christchurch I was angry that I had not been able to show New Zealand my true form. Now, in this game at Sydney, I was pulling out all the stops — and yet suddenly we were 11–0 down. Panic stations!

On a heavy ground the sprightly Australian full-back Arthur McGill had done well to kick his team into their healthy lead with two penalties and the conversion of a try by Phil Smith. Jarrett opened the Welsh score with a penalty goal before the close understanding which had developed between Gareth Edwards and his back row led to a try for Dai Morris.

GARETH EDWARDS: Once again I cannot speak too highly of Dai's effort. In contrasting style, the next score by Gerald Davies was just as great.

GERALD DAVIES: This try really gave me a big thrill. Having been put in possession 50 yards out with the full back to beat, I had to produce both speed and skill to reach the goal-line.
Keith Jarrett converted my try and also our next one by John Taylor, which I could probably have scored myself. I decided to make sure of it by feeding John. He had been a centre in his college days at Loughborough and fully understood how to provide his back division with an extra option in attack without ever getting in our way.

Jarrett's ten points this day were to be his last for Wales in a full International match before he left the amateur game for Barrow Rugby League club.
So the tourists had at last managed to show something of their true form. But they did not leave Sydney Oval without one final fright and a lesson about discipline. On the stroke of time McGill was awarded a try at the corner which prompted Maurice Richards and other Welsh players to argue fiercely with the referee, claiming the Wallaby had 'wriggled' after being held in a tackle. Mr Ferguson not only stuck to his decision but also gave Australia a penalty for dissent by Wales which, after McGill had converted his try, Alan Skinner attempted from half-way. The range, the mud and the occasion were too much for him, and Wales had won.

GARETH EDWARDS: This was an uncharacteristic outbreak by Maurice, and his hot-headedness could have cost us victory.
During my long career it came home to me again and again that whatever the circumstances it never, ever, pays to argue with the referee. He always holds the whip-hand — and a man who is penalized for dissent does a disservice to his fourteen team-mates.

Wales completed their trip with a festive match in Fiji and a 31–11 win. Many people subsequently asserted that the tourists would have been well advised to begin their programme in Fiji and Australia before venturing to challenge the All Blacks.

Keith Jarrett in action. A sensational place-kicker on his day, the Newport man turned professional on his return from Australia. In his last Test match he contributed ten points.

51

MATCH 18

24 January 1970 at Cardiff

WALES 6 (1T 1PG)
SOUTH AFRICA 6 (1T 1PG)

FACT BOX

This was the first time Wales avoided defeat at the Springboks' hands, South Africa having won all six previous encounters.

Wales J. P. R. Williams (Bridgend), P. Bennett, (Llanelli), S. J. Dawes (L. Welsh), W. H. Raybould (Newport), I. Hall (Aberavon), B. John (Cardiff), G. O. Edwards (Cardiff, Captain), D. Williams (Ebbw Vale), V. C. Perrins (Newport), D. B. Llewelyn (Newport), W. D. Thomas (Llanelli), T. G. Evans (L. Welsh), W. D. Morris (Neath), T. M. Davies (L. Welsh), D. Hughes (Newbridge).

South Africa H. O. de Villiers, S. H. Nomis, O. A. Roux, J. P. van der Merwe, G. Muller, M. J. Lawless, D. J. de Villiers (Captain), J. L. Myburgh, C. H. Cockrell, J. F. K. Marais, F. C. H. du Preez, I. J. de Klerk, P. J. F. Greyling, T. P. Bedford, J. H. Ellis.

SCORERS
Wales *Try* – Edwards; *Pen.* – Edwards.
South Africa *Try* – Nomis; *Pen.* – Henry de Villiers.

Referee: G. C. Lamb (RFU).

Because they have never defeated South Africa at rugby football Wales were, until 1981, when outside pressure became hard to resist, reluctant to call off fixtures with this controversy-racked nation: you don't quit while you are losing. Thus, despite incessant noises-off from anti-apartheid demonstrators who disrupted games during the Springboks' 1969–70 tour, the Cardiff Test duly got under way. Part of the new North Stand at 'The National Ground, Cardiff Arms Park' was opened for the occasion, but the playing area was sealed off by barbed wire and a cordon of uniformed policemen. Thus the game progressed without interruption, and the players' worst enemy turned out to

be the weather. For the last time — before use of the pitch was limited to official WRU fixtures — conditions were swamp-like.

Having lost to England and Scotland (not to mention Gwent and Newport RFC), and been held to a draw by Ireland, the tourists had every incentive to win this final representative fixture and regain some self-respect. Wales had been forced to reshuffle their back division after the decisions of Maurice Richards and Keith Jarrett to turn professional, and Llanelli RFC stand-off half Phil Bennett was selected as a wing.

PHIL BENNETT: I wasn't too happy at the prospect of marking Gert Muller, who had played against us at Stradey Park. A specialist wing with years of experience, he was big, strong and fast. However, I survived!

But I also tasted the deadly marking of International rugby. On one occasion I decided to beat the Springbok number 8 Tommy Bedford with the kind of side-step that would have left a club player for dead. Tommy never let me out of his sights and suddenly — bang! — I was on the deck.

The two sides looked evenly matched, but it was South Africa who took the lead. Barry John infringed the offside law at a scrummage near the Welsh posts, and H. O. de Villiers kicked a penalty.

BARRY JOHN: For days beforehand we had reminded ourselves that 'Larry' Lamb was particularly hot on this offence, and it was the one mistake we were all determined not to make. I must record my view that the referee was wrong.

Gareth Edwards's wide-angled penalty tied the score 3–3 at half-time, but again the Springboks nosed ahead, this time with a smartly executed blind-side move initiated by their captain Dawie de Villiers and finished off at the flag by Sid Nomis. The try showed how well the tourists had adapted to the appalling Atlantic coast weather, keeping the ball in front of their forwards until the backs could attack from short-range. Wales, in contrast, played as if the sun were shining: the backs' attempts to spin the ball led to knocks-on and other errors while Gareth Edwards, captaining the side, had much poorly directed possession to deal with behind his pack. However, the home side were not quite done for.

PHIL BENNETT: With time running out there was a ruck on the Welsh right, where the ball squirted back past Gareth Edwards. I nipped in and slung the ball out to Barry John.

GARETH EDWARDS: Barry's diagonal kick was a 'hoper', but it still landed perfectly just behind the South African midfield men. Ian Hall and Barry Llewelyn got quickly to the ball, and the latter tore it free and passed to me.

Just ten yards from the line, this was a moment of truth, for my troublesome hamstring had been nagging me in training. I cast caution to the wind and went for glory and my try earned us the draw.

I was disappointed not to get the range with my conversion attempt. But South Africa did not deserve to lose. They had overcome the wretched conditions far more successfully than Wales.

Barry John: **a hopeful diagonal kick which landed perfectly**.

BARRY JOHN: Many people remember how the Arms Park pitch, in the days when it was regularly used by Cardiff RFC and their reserve teams, could be like a paddy-field to play on. Few also realize, however, that in the depths of winter it smelt like a farmyard and tasted like an oil-well! Tractors had plied up and down it in the autumn spreading fertilizer to try and encourage a few blades of grass to grow. Once, when I fell on the ball, I got what can only be described as a dung-and-diesel cocktail!

53

7 February 1970 at Cardiff

WALES 18 (3G 1T)
SCOTLAND 9 (1T 1DG 1PG)

FACT BOX

Gordon Brown (West of Scotland) became the first man to replace a brother — Peter Brown (Gala) — during an international match.

Wales J. P. R. Williams (L. Welsh), L. T. D. Daniels (Newport), S. J. Dawes (L. Welsh), P. Bennett (Llanelli), I. Hall (Aberavon), B. John (Cardiff), G. O. Edwards (Cardiff, Captain), D. Williams (Ebbw Vale), V. C. Perrins (Newport), D. B. Llewelyn (Newport), W. D. Thomas (Llanelli), T. G. Evans (L. Welsh), W. D. Morris (Neath), T. M. Davies (L. Welsh), D. Hughes (Newbridge).

Scotland I. S. G. Smith, M. A. Smith, J. N. M. Frame, C. W. W. Rea, A. J. W. Hinshelwood, I. Robertson, R. G. Young, J. McLauchlan, F. A. L. Laidlaw, A. B. Carmichael, P. K. Stagg, P. C. Brown, W. Lauder, J. W. Telfer (Captain), R. J. Arneil. *Replacement:* G. L. Brown for Peter Brown.

SCORERS
Wales *Tries* – Daniel, Llewelyn, Dawes, Morris; *Cons.* – Edwards (2), Daniel.
Scotland *Try* – Robertson; *Pen.* – Lauder; *D.G.* – Robertson.

Referee: D. P. d'Arcy (IRFU).

If the Welsh had imagined that after ferocious encounters with the great Southern Hemisphere nations the defence of their European title would be straightforward, they had another think coming. Putting aside unhappy memories of an almost unbroken run of Cardiff defeats, the Scots used a strong wind to attack from the start and made their opponents pull out all the stops for victory.

BARRY JOHN: I felt great unease during this season and, along with other top players, was prevented by fatigue from hitting top form. After our return from the exhausting New Zealand tour, squad sessions for clubs, 'area' teams to meet the Springboks, and the National XV

seemed endless. Further, we kept being submitted to fitness training — of all things — when what we needed was novelty and innovation to revive our interest.

The Scots opened the scoring against a Welsh side in which Phil Bennett had moved in to partner John Dawes at centre and Laurie Daniel of Newport RFC had come in on the wing. Watsonian Ian Robertson dropped a goal after his forwards had heeled smoothly from a scrummage near their opponents' posts. Next came a penalty goal kicked by Wilson Lauder, a Scot brought up in Wales who played his club rugby with Neath RFC, and soon Scotland went 9–0 up when Robertson crossed for a try.

BARRY JOHN: I rate Ian's try one of the best ever scored by an opposite number of mine. Terrific footwork and sheer speed left us all for dead.

Big London Welshman Geoff Evans batters his way past Scotland's pack and looks for support.

With the chips down Denzil Williams called for a special effort from his pack, and the Welsh battled wholeheartedly to get back into contention. Against the breeze they would probably have settled for holding the Scots to a nine-point lead at the interval, but a bonus then presented itself in the shape of a try by new cap Laurie Daniel. He converted it himself, and although as it turned out he won no further caps, he could always look back with pride on an afternoon when he breathed fresh hope into his compatriots.

After the break the red forwards went from strength to strength, shoving Scotland back at the scrummages and winning three lines-out in every four. Barry Llewelyn was the first to exploit the visitors' ebbing resistance by bursting over from a loose scrum and reducing the deficit to a point; and then John Dawes pounced for a try when Robertson's clearing kick was charged down. As Gareth Edwards converted, the crowd realized that Wales were in the driving seat, and began singing their heroes home.

One more blow underlined the home team's superiority. A scrummage drive five yards from the Scottish line allowed Dai Morris to pick up and dive over for three points, which Edwards again turned into five. Wales now coasted in, well satisfied with a try-count of four to one.

This was a season when Gerald Davies decided to make himself unavailable for representative rugby football.

GERALD DAVIES: As a Cambridge undergraduate the demands of the University team, of Cardiff RFC in vacations and of Wales in our Triple Crown season, meant that I had experienced periods in 1969 when I was either travelling to play rugby, playing rugby, or returning from playing rugby. I had no time to involve myself in student life — which was, after all, why I had gone to Cambridge.

That is why I gave up International rugby, and looking back I think I got my priorities right. One must keep a sense of proportion.

28 February 1970 at Twickenham

ENGLAND 13 (2G 1PG)
WALES 17 (1G 3T 1DG)

FACT BOX

'Chico' Hopkins became the first Welsh replacement to score.

J. P. R. Williams was the third Welsh full back to score a try, following Vivian Jenkins and Keith Jarrett.

The four tries and 17 points by Wales at Twickenham were both records.

England R. B. Hiller (Captain), M. J. Novak, J. S. Spencer, D. J. Duckham, P. M. Hale, I. R. Shackleton, N. C. Starmer-Smith, C. B. Stevens, J. V. Pullin, K. E. Fairbrother, A. M. Davis, P. J. Larter, R. B. Taylor, B. R. West, A. L. Bucknall.

Wales J. P. R. Williams (L. Welsh), S. J. Watkins (Cardiff), W. H. Raybould (Newport), S. J. Dawes (L. Welsh), I. Hall (Aberavon), B. John (Cardiff), G. O. Edwards (Cardiff, Captain), D. Williams (Ebbw Vale), J. Young (Harrogate), D. B. Llewelyn (Newport), W. D. Thomas (Llanelli), T. G. Evans (L. Welsh), W. D. Morris (Neath), T. M. Davies (L. Welsh), D. Hughes (Newbridge). *Replacement:* R. Hopkins (Maesteg) for Gareth Edwards.

SCORERS
England *Tries* – Duckham, Novak; *Cons.* – Hiller (2); *Pen.* – Hiller.
Wales *Tries* – Mervyn Davies, John, J. P. R. Williams, Hopkins; *Con.* – J. P. R. Williams; *D.G.* – John.

Referee: R. Calmet (FRF).
Replaced by: R. F. Johnson (RFU).

Three points for the cheeky chappie! Replacement scrum half Ray Hopkins scores the fourth Welsh try. J. P. R. Williams's conversion climaxed an amazing come-back by the visitors.

Ray Hopkins of Maesteg RFC played just twenty minutes' rugby for his country. Seldom, however, can a sportsman have exploited so brief a period in his life to such devastating effect.

'Chico' took the field when a despondent Gareth Edwards limped down the tunnel nursing his tweaked hamstring, and leaving behind him an apparently beaten Welsh side who trailed 6–13. But

the cheeky replacement created one of the tries and scored the other, by which Wales recovered to snatch victory.

Smarting from their heavy defeat a year previously, England began as if it were their turn to score 30 points. After nine minutes' play J. P. R. Williams was caught in possession by new cap John Novak, whose supporting forwards won the ruck. Number 8 forward Bob Taylor made an extra man in midfield, drawing defenders before freeing David Duckham for a beautiful try which Bob Hiller converted. But Wales soon hit back through Mervyn Davies.

MERVYN DAVIES: To my amazement England left me unmarked at a line-out along their goal-line, where I had only to fall over and put the ball down.

This was one of only two tries that I scored for Wales. Playing with any other scrum half I might have picked up many more through close support play. But Gareth Edwards was so strongly-built that he could battle his way

past defenders who would have forced a weaker man to pass. So often I found myself empty-handed as Gareth powered his way to glory!

The home side struck again, moving the ball speedily to Novak, who ran in a try. Hiller kicked the conversion and a penalty to put his team ten points up at the break. During this respite referee Calmet of France — who had been accidentally enmeshed in a maul and cracked a shin-bone — surrendered his whistle to touch judge R. F. Johnson of the RFU, a fully qualified official.

Early in the second half another mistake by England — who were slow to gather a loose ball on their line — allowed Barry John to intervene and score. But from then on Wales battled unavailingly to make up the leeway. It was after a majestic attack by their opponents which swept 75 yards upfield that Edwards was left prone on the turf below the West Stand, clutching a thigh and clearly in pain. Off he went, and on came Hopkins.

J. P. R. WILLIAMS: England blew the game in that move of theirs. John Spencer got into our 25-area, but instead of passing to his unmarked wing he attempted to reach the line himself and allowed me to smother-tackle him.

No sooner had Chico come on than he and I brought off a move the Welsh squad had practised hard in training — a well-timed pass to the full back coming up hard on the blind side of a scrummage. A try is always a possibility in this situation, for the attacker is at full speed while the opposing full-back is at a standstill. Sure enough, I had too much momentum for Bob Hiller's tackle.

It seemed impossible, however, that England could be robbed of any more of the lead they had built so impressively earlier on. But they were.

At a line-out beneath the swelling sea of red on the old South Terrace a disastrous gap opened up between their back-row players, through which little Hopkins scuttled for Wales's fourth try. Even the thunderous applause which greeted his feat was muted compared with the tumult accompanying J. P. R. Williams's conversion. The unbelievable had happened: Wales were ahead.

A Barry John dropped goal brought down the curtain on what ranks among the most dramatic comebacks in rugby history.

14 March 1970 in Dublin

IRELAND 14 (1G 1T 1DG 1PG)
WALES 0

Ken Goodall . . . bursting upfield through the ranks of surprised opponents on his way to a superb try.

FACT BOX

Gareth Edwards and Barry John set a new Welsh record for half backs of 16 games together, beating that set between 1901 and 1910 by Dicky Owen and Dick Jones. Ireland's Tom Kiernan became his country's most capped player, with 47 appearances to his name.

Ireland T. J. Kiernan (Captain), A. T. A. Duggan, F. P. K. Bresnihan, C. M. H. Gibson, W. J. Brown, B. J. McGann, R. M. Young, P. O'Callaghan, K. W. Kennedy, S. Millar, W. J. McBride, M. G. Molloy, R. A. Lamont, K. G. Goodall, J. F. Slattery.

Wales J. P. R. Williams (L. Welsh), S. J. Watkins (Cardiff), S. J. Dawes (L. Welsh), W. H. Raybould (Newport), K. Hughes (Camb. Univ. and New Dock Stars), B. John (Cardiff), G. O. Edwards (Cardiff, Captain), D. Williams (Ebbw Vale), J. Young (Harrogate), D. B. Llewelyn (Newport), W. D. Thomas (Llanelli), T. G. Evans (L. Welsh), W. D. Morris (Neath), T. M. Davies (L. Welsh), D. Hughes (Newbridge).

SCORERS
Ireland Tries – Duggan, Goodall; Con. – Kiernan; Pen. – Kiernan; D.G. – McGann.

Referee: G. C. Lamb (RFU).

In big rugby, peaks and precipices are never far apart — as Wales were reminded in their Dublin bid for another Triple Crown.

During the 'seventies the Welsh were fond of claiming that even if several members of their team were having an off-day, one of the world-class men could always be relied upon for something special to save his side from defeat. But on this day at Lansdowne Road the *hwyl* engendered by Clive Rowlands's pre-match pep-talk evaporated before unrelenting Irish fire, while each and every one of the team proved fallible — Barry John, Gareth Edwards, Mervyn Davies, Dai Morris, even the consistent John Williams included.

J. P. R. WILLIAMS: We seemed the stronger team on paper. But you have to bear in mind that at the kick-off each side has a 50–50 chance. It only needs the favourites to play a bit below form and the under-dogs to rise above themselves — and the apple-cart is upset. That's especially true of International matches.

After an hour's play a lack-lustre game seemed headed for stalemate with Ireland apparently content to have contained the visitors. Wales looked to be settling for a draw, and a valuable away point in the Championship. Then the sky fell in.

The first Irishman to strike was stand-off Barry McGann, who put over a soaring dropped goal after fast scrummage possession. Soon Alan Duggan did well to pounce upon a dropped pass in the Welsh midfield, where full-back John Williams had come

up to join the attack. Duggan just won a thrilling race to the goal-line for an unconverted try.

Tom Kiernan kicked a penalty goal, but there remained one more moment of genius for Ireland to savour. This time it was number 8 forward Ken Goodall, covering dutifully, who collected an ill-directed kick-ahead by Barry John and burst upfield through the ranks of surprised Welshmen.

MERVYN DAVIES: His sheer momentum prevented any of us laying a hand on him, We thought John Williams would sort him out, but he beat our full-back with a neat overhead chip, caught the bounce and hared in for a superb try which Tom Kiernan converted.

As his opposite number I was doubly unhappy about this lapse, since Ken was a big rival for future Lions' tours. I was mightily relieved when he decided to turn professional!

J. P. R. WILLIAMS: This was a first Championship defeat for several of us, but I like to think that we took it well. Gerald Davies and I, for example, always made a special point of talking amicably with opponents who had beaten Wales, to show that we could take it.

MERVYN DAVIES: But our rugby-crazy supporters dreamed up some incredible excuses to explain away our beating. They said we had become big-headed. They said

we had been on the beer the night before. Some even alleged that Barry and Gareth had had a dressing-room punch-up before the match. Rubbish! We were just out-played on the day.

PHIL BENNETT: As a reserve I watched Barry and Gareth, in particular, have a nightmarish afternoon. But they were still picked for the next game. A decade later they might not have been so lucky. In the 1981 Welsh defeat at Murrayfield Gareth Davies and Brynmor Williams did not play all that badly. But by then the expectations of selectors and the Welsh public had been so heightened that the pair were kicked out.

However, the selectors of the day clearly thought that the brilliant Gareth Edwards was being in-hibited by the cares of the captaincy; so they now relieved him of it.

GARETH EDWARDS: For the first time in my Inter-national career I seriously feared that I was in danger of being dropped. One of our more vociferous and outspoken selectors, Jack Young, didn't help matters.

'Make the most of this evening, Gareth,' he said to me at the post-match banquet. 'You may not have another one like it.'

'If I'm out of the team, tell me straight away, Jack,' I retorted. 'Then I can get my fishing licence immediately!'

59

4 April 1970 at Cardiff
WALES 11 (1G 2PG)
FRANCE 6 (2T)

FACT BOX

Phil Bennett joined Alun Thomas (1951–52) as the only Welsh players to represent their country in three positions in one season. Bennett's appearance at stand off half followed games on the wing against South Africa and in the centre versus Scotland. Barry John had now scored three tries and five dropped goals for Wales (24 points); Gareth Edwards four tries, two conversions, a dropped goal and a penalty (22).
J. P. R. Williams (13 points) and Gerald Davies (9) were also making their presence felt.

Wales J. P. R. Williams (L. Welsh), J. L. Shanklin (L. Welsh), S. J. Dawes (L. Welsh, Captain), A. J. Lewis (Ebbw Vale), R. Mathias (Llanelli), P. Bennett (Llanelli), G. O. Edwards (Cardiff), D. J. Lloyd (Bridgend), J. Young (Harrogate), D. B. Llewelyn (Newport), W. D. Thomas (Llanelli), I. S. Gallacher (Llanelli), W. D. Morris (Neath), T. M. Davies (L. Welsh), J. Taylor (L. Welsh).
Replacement: W. H. Raybould (Newport) for Jim Shanklin.

France P. Villepreux, J. Cantoni, A. Marot, J-P. Lux, J-M. Bonal, L. Paries, M. Puget, J. Iracabal, R. Benesis, J-L. Azarete, J-P. Bastiat, E. Cester, J-P. Biemouret, B. Dauga, C. Carrere (Captain).

SCORERS
Wales *Try* – Morris; *Con.* – Williams; *Pens.* – Williams (2).
France *Tries* – Cantoni, Bonal.

Referee: K. D. Kelleher (IRFU).

The international career of John Dawes had hitherto been enigmatic. Fêted at Old Deer Park as the brain behind London Welsh's rise to glory, the Newbridge-born centre had played through only one representative season — 1964 — without being dropped by Wales. He seemed to be a man to whom the selectors turned only when D. K. Jones, Gerald Davies, Keith Jarrett, Billy Raybould or Ian Hall were unavailable. It may be that the restraint of his play and the artfulness of his scheming were lost on all but the most perceptive of onlookers.

GARETH EDWARDS: Nobody ever thought of John as a greyhound on the pitch. Yet I can never remember seeing the ball moved so speedily to our wings as when he was one of the centres.
In this game we became aware of another of his virtues — as captain he exercised a great steadying influence on some of the tearaways around him.

This then was the man chosen to rehabilitate Welsh self-respect and lead the challenge to France, who having dealt severely with Scotland and Ireland were now hunting a third scalp in their Championship campaign. Dawes found himself in charge of a team which had been radically overhauled. John Taylor, John Lloyd, Stuart Gallacher, Jim Shanklin, Roy Mathias and Arthur Lewis were introduced, while Phil Bennett made a first appearance for his country at stand-off half when injury forced Barry John to withdraw.

Refreshed after a two-month rest from International rugby, the French swung menacingly into action, pinning Wales in their own half. Skipper Carrère was here, there and everywhere, and soon the pressure he inspired yielded an unconverted try for Jean-Mari Bonal. It was against the run of play when John Williams kicked a penalty for the home side, and then added a second.

Under Dawes the Welsh were playing percentage rugby based on a big effort at forward.

GARETH EDWARDS: It was far too tight a game for the skipper to call for a London Welsh style running game. From close range I was well aware of the great work of our pack, in which John Taylor and new cap Stuart Gallacher were doing particularly well, and it was the latter's opportunism which led to our try. Louis Paries slung a careless pass towards Pierre Villepreux, Stuart intercepted, and good old Dai Morris was right there to take a scoring pass. J.P.R.'s conversion put us 11–3 up.

Now the voices of six thousand Frenchmen, the biggest complement ever to follow their team to Wales, began to demand more from the visitors. Giant number 8 forward Benoît Dauga was the man who responded. His break from the back of a scrummage sucked in the Welsh cover and released the Tricolours for a bout of uninhibited handling which ended with new cap Jacques Cantoni crossing for an unconverted try. It turned out to be the last score of the game.

Although Wales could not now lose their Championship title, the defeat in Ireland had made it likely that this season they must share it. And as expected, France overwhelmed England 35–13 a fortnight later to draw level on points. But John Dawes was already planning for 1971.

Championship Table 1969–70

	P	W	D	L	PF	PA	Pts
FRANCE (5)	4	3	0	1	60	33	6
WALES (1)	4	3	0	1	46	42	6
IRELAND (2)	4	2	0	2	33	28	4
ENGLAND (3)	4	1	0	3	40	69	2
SCOTLAND (4)	4	1	0	3	43	50	2

Evidence that even the game's great line-out jumpers are not averse to a tiny bit of illegal assistance! Below, it is Delme Thomas who wears the hot-pants!

Numbers in brackets indicate last season's positions.

16 January 1971 at Cardiff
WALES 22 (2G 1T 2DG 1PG)
ENGLAND 6 (1T 1PG)

A clash of titans out near touch: Jeremy Janion about to be halted by new Welsh cap John Bevan.

FACT BOX

For the first time since 1912 Wales took the lead in the series with England: 33–32, with 11 games drawn.
Gareth Edwards won his 20th cap.

Wales J. P. R. Williams (L. Welsh), T. G. R. Davies (L. Welsh), S. J. Dawes (L. Welsh, Captain), A. J. Lewis, (Ebbw Vale), J. C. Bevan (Cardiff), B. John (Cardiff), G. O. Edwards (Cardiff), D. Williams (Ebbw Vale), J. Young (Harrogate), D. B. Llewelyn (Llanelli), W. D. Thomas (Llanelli), M. G. Roberts (L. Welsh), M. G. Roberts (L. Welsh), J. Taylor (L. Welsh), T. M. Davies (L. Welsh), W. D. Morris (Neath).

England P. A. Rossborough, J. P. Janion, C. S. Wardlow, J. S. Spencer, D. J. Duckham, I. D. Wright, J. J. Page, D. L. Powell, J. V. Pullin, K. E. Fairbrother, B. F. Ninnes, P. J. Larter, A. L. Bucknall (Captain), R. C. Hannaford, A. Neary.

SCORERS
Wales Tries – Gerald Davies (2), Bevan; Cons. – Taylor (2); Pen. – Williams; D. Gs. – John (2).
England Try – Hannaford; Pen. – Rossborough.

Referee: D. P. d'Arcy (IRFU).

January 1971 saw the start of an international season in which England dearly wanted success to accompany the Centenary of the Rugby Football Union. Given that aim, it seemed foolhardy of their selectors to choose seven new caps for the opening encounter at Cardiff. Tony Bucknall's team was to meet the same rude fate as its three precursors — for the Welsh were not willing to stand on ceremony.

Yet another London Welshman had been introduced to serve under John Dawes, the burly Denbighshire-bred lock Mike Roberts. Gerald Davies, his Cambridge rugby days over, had transferred to Old Deer Park, and was again available for representative rugby, while John Bevan on the opposite wing was the latest Rhondda Valley product to pull on the red jersey of Wales.

A skilled, well-drilled home eight were quick to gain a supremacy which they never surrendered, prompting the comment from veteran critic Vivian Jenkins that no Welsh pack had performed better while he had been reporting the game. Their half-backs revelled in swift, high-quality possession, and within nine minutes Barry John had dropped a goal.

BARRY JOHN: Playing with John Dawes at my elbow was good for me. While not condoning anything ill-considered, he still gave me every encouragement to express myself.

England number 8 Charlie Hannaford soon swooped for an unconverted try at the end of a line-out, but this was a mere stumble on Wales's

triumphant march. Hitting its stride, the Welsh back division began to look as accomplished a unit as its forwards. Gerald Davies scored a fine try which John Taylor converted from close to touch. John Dawes plotted, schemed and master-minded switches of direction. The dazzling all-round ability of Barry John drew roars of appreciation — and soon set up a try for the Cardiff College of Education student John Bevan.

BARRY JOHN: This move gave me tremendous satisfaction. I picked up a loose ball inside our half close to the North Stand touch-line and began running upfield. To beat the England defender who confronted me, I side-footed the ball along the ground to his left, dodging around him the other way myself. Crossing from touch back into the playing area I regained possession and found John handily placed for a scoring pass. The crowd seemed to love it!

Then the attacking emphasis swung back to the other wing, where Gerald Davies contributed another try which John Taylor converted.

Just before the interval Jeremy Janion knocked on with the Welsh line at his mercy, but that was the last time for the home team to offer the opposition a chance. Equally, their lust for points seemed to ebb, and they appeared content to remain firmly in control of the exchanges. Hence no try was scored in the second period, when John Williams kicked a penalty, Barry John almost casually put over a second dropped goal, and Peter Rossborough had the satisfaction of notching a penalty for England in his first International match.

BARRY JOHN: In this game we realized that we had become a formidable team, and were well captained.

Afterwards it was revealed that John Williams had played for seventy-five minutes with a depressed fracture of the cheekbone. People saw this as another pointer to the full-back's courage and indifference to pain.

J. P. R. WILLIAMS: I banged my face against the hard head of Gareth Edwards as we both tried to catch a high ball, but simply thought I had been bruised. Not until the Monday did a colleague at St Mary's take a close look and decide that I needed a minor operation.

MATCH 24

6 February 1971 at Murrayfield

SCOTLAND 18 (2T 4PG)
WALES 19 (2G 2T 1PG)

John Taylor was a very gifted all-round rugby player. Blessed with good powers of anticipation, he was a sturdy tackler who could run and handle like a back. Yet the first of his achievements to be recalled in any conversation between keen followers of the game is the conversion kick which clinched victory for his team after a desperately close contest in Edinburgh, and kept Wales firmly on course for a Grand Slam.

Because of its climax many senior Welsh players regard this match as the most exciting in which they have ever played (they include Ian Hall, who joined an otherwise unchanged XV in the centre instead of the injured Arthur Lewis). For openers, Peter Brown kicked two penalties against one by Barry John before the game burst into flower: John Williams surged forward on a run which included a fine dummy and body-swerve before transferring to John Taylor.

MERVYN DAVIES: John still had two defenders to beat, and did very well to reach the line for a try which Barry John converted.

John and Dai Morris formed, with myself, the best back row I ever played in. Both attackers by nature, they loved to get forward fast. I would move just behind them to guard against any danger that threatened as a result.

Another inch or two of height would have made John more effective at the line-out. But this was never vital because of my own ball-winning ability.

Soon after the interval Gareth Edwards advanced the Welsh lead to 11–6 when he powered around the blind side of a ruck. But now Scotland's forwards — who were giving a better account of themselves than had England's at Cardiff — produced something special, and Sandy Carmichael burst across for a try after the visitors' failure to control line-out possession near their corner flag. The home side regained the lead through a third Peter Brown penalty.

A break by John Bevan gave Barry John space to side-step and shimmy his way over for a try, but after being shaken up in the final tackle the stand-off misjudged his conversion attempt. Still neither side was counting any chickens, even when Peter Brown cracked over his fourth penalty. But Murrayfield did reach boiling-point when a mistake by John Bevan, compounded by hesitation in the Welsh midfield, allowed the speedy Chris Rea in for a try half-way between posts and corner flag. This time Brown's conversion kick hit a post, but Scotland were still four points ahead.

The stage was set for a grandstand finish, which came from Wales. According to some Welsh players, Scotland's line-out instructions were misunderstood by the thrower-in five minutes from time. Certainly Delme Thomas was given precious space to palm down the ball, for Gareth Edwards to send the backs off on a do-or-die run.

GERALD DAVIES: John Williams came perfectly into the line and floated a pass which allowed me to get well outside my wing and reach the goal-line. I began heading for the posts, but the Scottish cover forced me to touch down about 15 yards from the corner flag.

Some of the visiting players could not bear to watch Taylor's kick at goal, but a huge roar from their supporters soon proclaimed that he had got everything right. A high, straight, handsome conversion

brought him the most important two points in Welsh rugby history.

MERVYN DAVIES: All's well that ends well, but when John's kick went over I must have been the most relieved Welshman in Edinburgh. I knew only too well that I had handed Scotland two of their penalties on a plate — one for getting offside, the other for failing to release the ball after a tackle.

John Taylor: a huge roar from the Welsh supporters announced that he had got everything right and claimed the most important two points in Welsh rugby history.

13 March 1971 at Cardiff

WALES 23 (1G 3T 1DG 2PG)
IRELAND 9 (3PG)

Making a record 35th appearance as a Welsh forward, Denzil Williams delivers the ball to Gareth Edwards. . . . Five years later Williams himself would be overtaken by Mervyn Davies *(right foreground)*.

FACT BOX

Denzil Williams broke Bryn Meredith's record as the most-capped Welsh forward, winning a 35th cap in a game when Wales captured their 12th Triple Crown.
The Ebbw Vale prop, frequently a lock for his club, played in all the Triple Crown games during the 1965, 1969 and 1971 seasons.

Wales J. P. R. Williams (L. Welsh), T. G. R. Davies (L. Welsh), S. J. Dawes (L. Welsh, Captain), A. J. Lewis (Ebbw Vale), J. C. Bevan (Cardiff), B. John (Cardiff), G. O. Edwards (Cardiff), D. Williams (Ebbw Vale), J. Young (Harrogate), D. B. Llewelyn (Llanelli), W. D. Thomas (Llanelli), M. G. Roberts (L. Welsh), J. Taylor (L. Welsh), T. M. Davies (L. Welsh), W. D. Morris (Neath).

Ireland B. J. O'Driscoll, A. T. A. Duggan, C. M. H. Gibson (Captain), F. P. K. Bresnihan, E. L. Grant, B. J. McGann, R. M. Young, R. J. McLoughlin, K. W. Kennedy, J. F. Lynch, W. J. McBride, M. G. Molloy, M. L. Hipwell, D. J. Hickie, J. F. Slattery.

SCORERS
Wales *Tries* — Gerald Davies (2), Edwards (2); *Con.* — John; *Pens.* — John (2); *D.G.* — John.
Ireland *Pens.* — Gibson (3).

Referee: R. F. Johnson (RFU).

On this Triple Crown day Gareth Edwards and Barry John were everything they had not been in Dublin a year earlier. The former, by a season the junior partner, turned in a game which emphasized the colossal strides he had made in four seasons of International play.

GARETH EDWARDS: With very few exceptions, such as Haydn Tanner, scrum-halves had always been mainly regarded as feeders of the backs — which is why from 1968 on I worked hard to perfect a pass which would satisfy critics, selectors and my outside-half.

But from schooldays, when I often played at centre, I always wanted to be more than just a link-man. Like the other backs, I craved chances to run with the ball, and score if possible. This was one of the games when I managed to play a dual role.

Outside Edwards, Barry John was the field-marshal, surveying the scene coolly before deciding where Ireland might be vulnerable to a tactical probe. After contributing 17 of Wales's points in a win which clinched another Triple Crown the pair were borne shoulder-high from the field by delirious spectators who chanted, 'We are the Champions'.

Welsh supremacy, however, began up front with the gradual subduing of an Irish pack which would supply several men to the British Isles tour party that summer. Pack leader Denzil Williams — now near to the end of his International career — could

take much of the credit for this inspiring display.

Arthur Lewis was back in a Welsh side which at this time often appeared to begin in too low a gear, and there were the usual groans from the Cardiff crowd when Ireland went six-up through two Mike Gibson penalty goals. The home side now galvanized itself to action, spurred on by a beautiful Gerald Davies try.

GERALD DAVIES: Acceleration and pace-change did the damage fifteen yards out, and by the time I crossed Ireland's line there was scarcely a defender in sight.

After a game like this, when we each scored twice, people used to ask if Gareth Edwards and I were having a personal try race. At this stage in our careers, we weren't. Perhaps a little rivalry had crept in by 1975 and 1976 when the media focused sharply on our neck-and-neck progress!

Although Barry John found the range with a dropped goal and a penalty to give Wales a 9–6 lead at the interval, there was to be no quick surrender by the Irish, and twenty-five more minutes went by before Wales moved out of reach. Then it was Edwards who opened the floodgates with a try set up by Barry Llewelyn, and a scoring pass delivered minutes later to Gerald Davies. Gibson broke the sequence with a penalty, only for John to respond with a superb shot from 50 yards. Finally he converted a second try by Edwards.

GARETH EDWARDS: People may remember that I slammed the ball down hard over the Irish goal-line. This was my instinctive retort to the public and the Press, who seemed to have been riding me non-stop for twelve months. I had grown up as a rugby man, and learned an important lesson: if the media seem unfair, the best place to hit back is on the field. That's how you make them eat their words!

I knew I would score this try from the moment I got possession at the end of a line-out. A determined drive past the back row, a shrug of the hips to shake off tenacious Mike Gibson, and there was the line!

Shortly after this game the Lions party for New Zealand was announced. Managed by Dr Douglas Smith and coached by Carwyn Jones, it contained eleven of the Welsh team which had beaten Ireland.

67

MATCH 26

27 March 1971 at Stade Colombes

FRANCE 5 (1G)
WALES 9 (2T 1PG)

After a gap of nineteen years Wales completed the Grand Slam with a win in Paris which many observers rate the best all-round display given by the men in red since the Second World War. John Dawes's team outscored their opponents in tries, and also provided a tremendous account of themselves in defence against a French XV to whom victory would have given a share of the title.

68

France — playing scintillating rugby from the outset — opened the scoring with a Benoît Dauga try converted by Pierre Villepreux. It was only thanks to non-stop covering and tackling by Mervyn Davies, John Taylor and Dai Morris in the Welsh back row that the visitors did not fall further behind. Barry John showed bravery in a try-saving tackle upon Dauga which gave the Welshman a broken nose, and forced him briefly from the field for attention.

He returned to join a defence that was yet again at full stretch, this time to contain a superb move on the French right which sent wing Roger Bourgarel speeding into the Welsh 25-area.

J. P. R. WILLIAMS: Because John Taylor had Bourgarel covered I risked going for the interception, caught an inside pass, and was on my way upfield with only two Frenchmen in a position to catch me. My only support seemed to be prop Denzil Williams, who was running out of steam, but suddenly I glimpsed Gareth Edwards behind me and to the left. I checked the two coverers with an inside jink and fed my team-mate, who just reached the corner. How he got into the right place at the right time I will never know!

Although this magnificent score went unconverted, Barry John put Wales into the lead soon after half-time with a penalty goal. Then, after Wales had achieved a midfield attacking position on the French 25-line, the stand-off half got the try which made the match safe.

Barry John: an all-round display that gave much satisfaction.

BARRY JOHN: Full marks first to our hooker Jeff Young for taking the ball against the head at a set scrummage. It meant that France's defenders, including my opposite number Berot, were fractionally out of position and I had room to aim my run at inside-centre Bertranne. He must have thought I intended feeding John Dawes, and kept moving outwards. So my last-second change of direction allowed me to get between the two and reach the line, with Berot's finger-tips clutching for my jersey. That was the big moment of a game in which I had given an all-round display that pleased me very much. It even eased the pain of my aching nose!

The exchanges continued to be fierce, but France never thereafter threatened to draw level, and at the final whistle it was John Dawes's turn to be chaired from the field.

Skipper John Dawes was chaired from the field.

Championship Table 1970–71

	P	W	D	L	PF	PA	Pts
WALES (1)	4	4	0	0	73	38	8
FRANCE (1)	4	1	2	1	41	40	4
ENGLAND (4)	4	1	1	2	44	58	3
IRELAND (3)	4	1	1	2	41	46	3
SCOTLAND (4)	4	1	0	3	47	64	2

Numbers in brackets indicate last season's positions.

15 July 1972 at Twickenham

ENGLAND 3 (1PG)
WALES 12 (1G 2PG)

Having led the Lions triumphantly in New Zealand John Dawes had now left International rugby, as had Denzil Williams. Thus for the first encounter of the 1972 campaign the Welsh selectors killed two birds with one stone, bringing in John Lloyd of Bridgend at prop, and making him captain. Roy Bergiers of Llanelli RFC came in at centre, and Geoff Evans of London Welsh returned at lock.

MERVYN DAVIES: After the Grand Slam by Wales and our Test series victory in New Zealand this match seemed an anticlimax. Not that we were ever in danger of defeat — the very idea of losing to England was impossible to entertain. But our top players were certainly not at concert pitch after their post-tour lay-off.

There seemed no reason why this new-look side should not pick up where John Dawes's team had left off, but in the event a determined England combination under Bob Hiller put up sterner opposition than had been expected. In the first half they performed particularly well, without producing the finishing power to crack a resolute Welsh defence.

Lapses of concentration, however, allowed Barry John to put over a pair of penalty goals. Hiller, his place-kicking style a total contrast with that of his Welsh rival, kept his side in the hunt with a good reply, while the assured play of new caps like Jan Webster, Mike Burton and the tall, lean Andy Ripley led their supporters to hope that more points were on the way.

The interval arrived without any sign that the Welsh were in barnstorming mood. Their pack had achieved parity in all aspects of the play, but although the backs were in satisfactory form as individuals they seemed to miss the cementing capability of John Dawes.

Nevertheless, they were in charge of the game, and made sure of victory with another Twickenham 'special' by John Williams in the second half.

J. P. R. WILLIAMS: My try was a carbon-copy of the one scored in 1970, except that this time Gareth Edwards was at scrum-half to set it up.

He was so strong that he could draw a whole back row on to him, and when he slipped me the ball on the blind side I had only Hiller to beat. Once more, with his heels on the England goal-line, he was on a hiding to nothing. Barry John got the extra points with a good conversion.

This season the try had been revalued from three to four points, so the lead was now a comfortable 12–3. Welsh hearts leaped to their mouths, however, at one juncture shortly before the end. The brilliant David Duckham eluded his opposite number, and wrong-footing the Welsh back-row cover, bore down on the solitary remaining defender, John Williams. But the big side-step with which he tried to beat the full-back foundered upon the greasy turf, and with it perished England's last hope of saving the game. Wales had won a low-key match.

J. P. R. WILLIAMS: I liked most things about Twickenham except its playing surface. Because of too much use its quality was uneven, like that of Lansdowne Road and Newlands in South Africa. My favourite pitches were Murrayfield and Cardiff Arms Park.

Barry Llewelyn (centre) **about to take a pass from fellow-prop John Lloyd, captaining Wales for the first time. His team met sterner oppostion than they had expected.**

5 February 1972 at Cardiff
WALES   35 (3G 2T 3PG)
SCOTLAND 12 (1G 2PG)

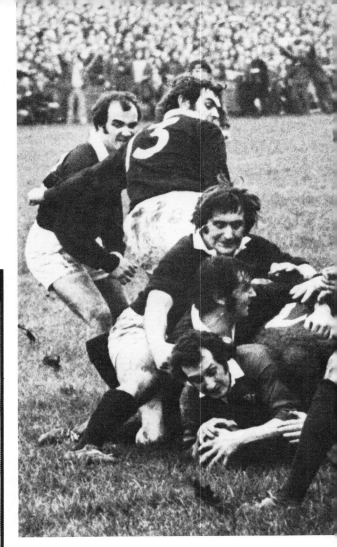

Not *the* spectacular try by Gareth Edwards — which will never be forgotten by those who saw it. But this was the one, claims the scrum half himself, which swung the game Wales's way.

FACT BOX

Wales registered their biggest-ever score versus Scotland and a record winning margin of 23 points.

Wales   J. P. R. Williams (L. Welsh), T. G. R. Davies (L. Welsh), R. T. E. Bergiers (Llanelli), A. J. Lewis (Ebbw Vale), J. C. Bevan (Cardiff), B. John (Cardiff), G. O. Edwards (Cardiff), D. J. Lloyd (Bridgend, Captain), J. Young (RAF), D. B. Llewelyn (Llanelli), T. G. Evans (L. Welsh), W. D. Thomas (Llanelli), W. D. Morris (Neath), T. M. Davies (L. Welsh), J. Taylor (L. Welsh).
Replacement: P. Bennett (Llanelli) for J. P. R. Williams.

Scotland   A. R. Brown, W. C. C. Steele, J. N. M. Frame, J. M. Renwick, A. G. Biggar, C. M. Telfer, D. S. Paterson, A. B. Carmichael, R. L. Clark, J. McLauchlan, I. A. Barnes, G. L. Brown, N. A. MacEwan, R. J. Arneil, P. C. Brown (Captain).
Replacement: L. G. Dick for Biggar.

SCORERS
Wales   *Tries* – Edwards (2), Gerald Davies, Bergiers, Taylor; *Cons.* – John (3); *Pens.* – John (3).
Scotland   *Try* – Clark; *Con.* – Peter Brown; *Pens.* – Brown, Renwick.

Referee: G. A. Jamieson (IRFU).

Before their own supporters Wales recovered top form, and ultimately showed no mercy to a Scottish XV which had looked strong on paper and stayed in contention until the final quarter. It took a great performance by Gareth Edwards to place the result beyond doubt, with the second of his two tries standing as perhaps the finest solo feat ever accomplished in a Welsh jersey.

After Peter Brown and Barry John had exchanged penalties Gerald Davies contributed what would normally have been the score of the match. Outstripping Biggar, he used a clever chip ahead to beat the defence and get a try which gave Wales the lead. Further penalties from Brown and John saw the home team just ahead at the end of a half in which John Williams and Biggar retired with mouth and hamstring injuries respectively. Phil Bennett and Louis Dick were the replacements.

Scotland's hooker Clark now scored a corner try which was beautifully converted by Brown before Edwards turned on the power. First came a try from short range.

GARETH EDWARDS: Barry Llewelyn peeled away from a line-out, only to be held up a yard short of the goal-line. It was sheer determination, added to the gym-

nastic ability which I mentioned before, that enabled me to take his pass and get over the line.

That try was probably the more important of the two I got in this match. It took much steam out of Scotland and swung the game our way again. But the one that came next was the most pleasurable I ever scored!

It began with my getting the ball at a scrummage near our 25-line, at which point the idea of scoring never entered my mind! Looking back, I divide it into four stages:

Stage one: I get away from the Scottish back row. A surprise — because I was expecting to be nailed by flanker Roger Arneil.

Stage two: Confidently I anticipate support from Dai Morris. But glancing round, I find that for once he is not there — I am on my own! However, I have covered ten yards: let's see how far I can go.

Stage three: Still without close support I am confronted by Scotland's full back, whom I beat with a chip over his head. Now the goal-line is just 30 yards away, and my objective is to control the ball with my feet. A left-footed jab sends it flying towards the corner flag. Can I reach it before it rolls into touch? For once I am aware of the crowd roaring me on.

Stage four: The ball seems to be pulling up in just the right spot, but Scotland's right wing, covering desperately from the far side of the field, threatens to beat me to the touch-down. This is the climax, and I tell myself that I haven't run all this way to lose the race at the last second. Will-power comes into it, and I *choose* to get there first. . . . Try!

Back at school Bill Samuel always used to order, 'If the chance is there, go for it *hard*.' I hope he approved.

Roy Bergiers was next to score — his first International try — after which John Taylor gave a virtuoso turn of his own, selling the dummy to a bunch of defenders and crossing for the fifth Welsh try. Punctuating these events were penalty goals and conversions by Barry John which gave him a personal haul for the match of 15 points. Wales had avenged their 1924 defeat at Inverleith, when Scotland also ran up 35 points.

25 March 1972 at Cardiff

WALES 20 (2T 4PG)
FRANCE 6 (2PG)

FACT BOX

On his 25th and last appearance for Wales, Barry John became the most prolific scorer for his country in internationals. Reaching 90 points (five tries, six conversions, eight dropped goals and 13 penalties) he overtook Jack Bancroft's 88 set in 1909–14.

John also broke the record he shared with Keith Jarrett for most points in a season (31), registering 35 in only three games.

The stand off half, who was to announce his retirement from rugby football on May 7, also finished with Welsh records for dropped goals (8) and penalty goals (13).

Gerald Davies also reached milestones in this game, winning his 20th cap and scoring his tenth try.

Wales J. P. R. Williams (L. Welsh), T. G. R. Davies (L. Welsh), R. T. E. Bergiers (Llanelli), A. J. Lewis (Ebbw Vale), J. C. Bevan (Cardiff), B. John (Cardiff), G. O. Edwards (Cardiff), D. J. Lloyd (Bridgend, Captain), J. Young (RAF), D. B. Llewelyn (Llanelli), T. G. Evans (L. Welsh), W. D. Thomas (Llanelli), W. D. Morris (Neath), T. M. Davies (L. Welsh), J. Taylor (L. Welsh).
Replacement: D. L. Quinnell (Llanelli) for Mervyn Davies.

France P. Villepreux (Captain), B. Duprat, J. Maso, J-P. Lux, J. Sillieres, J-L. Berot, M. Barrau, J. Iracabal, R. Benesis, J-L. Azarete, A. Esteve, C. Spanghero, J-C. Skrela, B. Dauga, J-P. Biemouret.

SCORERS
Wales *Tries* – Gerald Davies, Bevan; *Pens.* – John (4).
France *Pens.* – Villepreux (2).

Referee: M. H. Titcomb (RFU).

Because of the Troubles, Scotland and Wales declined to play in Ireland this season. The Welsh decision, reached after consultations with the players, may have robbed them of another Grand Slam. But Irish frustration was no less, Tom Kiernan's men having won precious away victories at Colombes and Twickenham. They too considered themselves robbed of a tilt at a Grand Slam.

It was thus eight weeks since the defeat of Scotland when France arrived in Cardiff to meet an unchanged home team, John Williams having recovered from surgery to his teeth and jaw. For once the visitors did not seem to present an extraordinary threat, for despite a 37–12 win over England, their record showed defeats at the hands of Ireland and Scotland. But Pierre Villepreux reminded Wales that victory had still to be worked for with two prodigious penalty goals from 60 yards' range (later in the match he just missed a third from the same distance).

The consistent Barry John put over two of his own, before completing a hat-trick to gain his side a half-time lead. His tactical kicking was also valuable in this his last game for Wales.

BARRY JOHN: One advantage of having a reputation is that opponents stand in awe of you! By holding back to cover possible breaks they give you space to kick with extra precision. Sometimes they put more tacklers on you — so, as Steve Heighway used to do for Bill Shankly's Liverpool side, you 'take out two' and create more room for team-mates.

PHIL BENNETT: One of his penalty goals this day summed up the amazing confidence of my predecessor in the Welsh XV — I suppose it bordered on arrogance.

He planted the ball, trotted back with a casual glance at the sky as if to sense the wind direction, and then placed the goal from long range. He gave me the feeling that even if the attempt had missed he would have said to himself, 'So what? I'll score a try instead.'

As the second half got under way the Welsh slowly gained their expected supremacy. Up front the pack won its battle and sapped the opposition's will to cover, thus ensuring space for the backs to employ their tricks. John Bevan was first to exploit the situation. Put in possession a yard inside French territory, he broke past several defenders and raced on towards Villepreux. Avoiding a confrontation with the full-back, he punted over his head, just managing to control the ball on its descent and cross for an outstanding try.

Barry John's conversion attempt was wide, but he quickly kicked a compensating penalty to break a long-standing record (see below). Next he combined with Arthur Lewis to offer the ghost of a chance to Gerald Davies. The wing seemed certain to be overwhelmed by French defenders, but somehow he bobbed and weaved his way between them to reach

the line. Their win put Wales on top of the never-to-be-completed Championship table.

A couple of weeks later, after a final Cardiff Arms Park appearance in a charity match, Barry John announced his retirement from the game.

PHIL BENNETT: In my experience, a number of backs were faster than Barry over 50 yards. But he had an incredible change of pace that made him a nightmare to mark. He would draw an opponent into the tackle before gliding effortlessly from his grasp.

As team-mates and opponents we had lots of laughs. I used to pull his leg about 'Hollywooding' — that is, acting up to get a penalty for a late tackle that he didn't really deserve. He always claimed with a grin that he'd had the finest teacher in the land — George Best!

A great try by Gerald Davies prevents France's Sillieres from scoring at the corner. The Welshman (a) uses great speed to overtake his prey; (b) applies a smothered tackle; (c) uses body strength to turn the Frenchman; (d) rolls him into touch.

Championship Table 1971–72

	P	W	D	L	PF	PA	Pts
WALES (1)	3	3	0	0	67	21	6
IRELAND (3)	2	2	0	0	30	21	4
SCOTLAND (5)	3	2	0	1	55	53	4
FRANCE (2)	4	1	0	3	61	66	2
ENGLAND (3)	4	0	0	4	36	88	0

Numbers in brackets indicate last season's positions. Championship uncompleted because neither Scotland nor Wales felt they could visit Dublin with the increase in violence in Northern Ireland and the threat of sabotage in the South.

2 December 1972 at Cardiff

WALES 16 (1T 4PG)
NEW ZEALAND 19 (1T 5PG)

FACT BOX

New Zealand were the first visiting country to win at Cardiff since France in 1968.

Wales J. P. R. Williams (Bridgend), T. G. R. Davies (L. Welsh), R. T. E. Bergiers (Llanelli), J. L. Shanklin (L. Welsh), J. C. Bevan (Cardiff), P. Bennett (Llanelli), G. O. Edwards (Cardiff), G. Shaw, (Neath), J. Young (L. Welsh), D. B. Llewelyn (Llanelli), W. D. Thomas (Llanelli, Captain), D. L. Quinnell (Llanelli), W. D. Morris (Neath), T. M. Davies (Swansea), J. Taylor (L. Welsh).

New Zealand J. F. Karam, B. G. Williams, D. A. Hales, R. M. Parkinson, G. B. Batty, R. E. Burgess, S. M. Going, J. D. Matheson, R. W. Norton, K. Murdoch, H. H. MacDonald, P. J. Whiting, A. J. Wyllie, A. R. Sutherland, I. A. Kirkpatrick (Captain).
Replacement: A. I. Scown for Wyllie.

SCORERS
Wales *Try* – Bevan; *Pens.* – Bennett (4).
New Zealand *Try* – Murdoch; *Pens.* – Karam (5).

Referee: R. F. Johnson (RFU).

For the first time New Zealand television viewers, glued to their sets in the early hours of the morning, were able to watch live satellite transmission of the All Blacks at play in Europe. They went to bed happy, having seen the tourists beat off a late rally by Wales to win a battle of penalty goals.

Although injury forced the withdrawal of captain-designate Arthur Lewis (replaced by Delme Thomas), the home team contained many survivors from the previous winter's unbeaten campaign. Phil Bennett was a logical and tested successor to the departed Barry John, and the only new cap was Neath prop Glyn Shaw. For all that, Wales found themselves six points down within ten minutes as a

result of elementary errors which New Zealand full-back Joe Karam punished with penalty goals.

GARETH EDWARDS: Often Wales allowed England or another European team to score first, and then overhauled them later. The All Blacks were different. Once they got their noses in front they were going to keep things that way. They were quick to take this game by the scruff of the neck.

The visitors pressed home their advantage with a try by Keith Murdoch, the controversial prop who was sent home following an incident in a Cardiff hotel the same night. Given possession at a line-out, Sid Going hoisted a kick into the Welsh 25. Following up, he put defender John Bevan under immediate pressure, recovered the ball, and sent Murdoch slithering in close to the corner flag. Karam's conversion attempt failed, but at 10–0 up New Zealand already looked home and dry. Phil Bennett kicked Wales's first three points with a penalty — to which Karam soon replied.

GARETH EDWARDS: Every time we clawed back a few points, New Zealand proved capable of re-establishing their lead. It was like running up a sandhill.

Shortly after the interval Gareth Edwards disrupted the opposing half-backs, and Bennett was at hand to play the ball to John Bevan. With the All Black defence drawn infield the wing had just enough pace and space to reach the corner for a spectacular try. It went unconverted, but the deficit was now six points. Bennett kicked two more penalty goals; but inevitably — if somewhat against the run of play — Karam preserved the lead with two for New Zealand.

Containment now became the the visitors' aim, as with twenty minutes left the Welsh threw everything into attack. Soon Cardiff Arms Park erupted as John Williams came up to join an attack and force his way across the All Black line. Referee Johnson, however, disallowed the score for alleged 'wriggling'.

GARETH EDWARDS: Maybe Mr Johnson was swayed by the instantly voiced opinion of Sid Going, who never missed a chance of indulging in gamesmanship.

J. P. R. WILLIAMS: I scored all right — my own momentum carried me across the goal-line. But as I got up from under a pile of players the referee told me tersely, 'You crawled over.' I kept my mouth shut at the time, for it never pays to argue with a referee. But I have no hesitation in saying now that Mr Johnson was wrong.

A tremendous shame, for if that try had been awarded I am sure we would have gone on to win.

GARETH EDWARDS: By this stage in the match, New Zealand were out on their feet.

As the game drew to a close the tourists resorted to obstructive tactics to check the manœuvres of the Welsh backs, but all they conceded was a final penalty kicked by Bennett. After five successive victories in the long series between the two nations, it seemed that New Zealand had laid the Welsh bogy.

GARETH EDWARDS: So often New Zealand seem to catch Wales in a trough between great periods. Certainly this was true in the 'seventies. Both in 1972 and 1978, for instance, we had just lost key players, and their successors were not yet battle-hardened.

But you have to hand it to the 'Blacks'. They are always well-organized and difficult to beat, even with the sort of disciplinary problems off the field that the team of 1972 experienced.

Stewards are about to remove the figure 16 from its slot *(background)* in the fond hope that this last-minute penalty attempt by Phil Bennett will tie the scores at 19–19. But the Llanelli man just fails to draw the ball in from outside the near post, and the All Blacks hold on to win.

20 January 1973 at Cardiff

WALES 25 (1G 4T 1PG)
ENGLAND 9 (1DG 2PG)

FACT BOX

By registering a fifth successive win over England, Wales equalled the records of 1903 and 1909.

Wales J. P. R. Williams (L. Welsh), T. G. R. Davies (L. Welsh), R. T. E. Bergiers (Llanelli), A. J. Lewis (Ebbw Vale, Captain), J. C. Bevan (Cardiff), P. Bennett (Llanelli), G. O. Edwards (Cardiff), G. Shaw (Neath), J. Young (L. Welsh), D. J. Lloyd (Bridgend), W. D. Thomas (Llanelli), D. L. Quinnell (Llanelli), J. Taylor (L. Welsh), T. M. Davies (Swansea), W. D. Morris (Neath).

England S. A. Doble, A. J. Morley, P. J. Warfield, P. S. Preece, D. J. Duckham, A. R. Cowman, J. G. Webster, F. E. Cotton, J. V. Pullin (Captain), C. B. Stevens, C. W. Ralston, P. J. Larter, A. Neary, A. G. Ripley, J. A. Watkins. *Replacement:* G. W. Evans for Warfield.

SCORERS
Wales *Tries* – Bevan (2), Gerald Davies, Edwards, Lewis; *Con.* – Bennett; *Pen.* – Taylor.
England *Pens.* – Doble (2); *D.G.* – Cowman.

Referee: G. Domercq (FRF).

An 'Arthur' brings a try for skipper Arthur Lewis; 'a move needing great courage and commitment.'

Showing no signs of reaction after their defeat by New Zealand, Wales applied themselves to the defence of a European title which they had held in effect since 1971. Arthur Lewis and John Lloyd returned to the fray at the expense of Jim Shanklin and Glyn Shaw, and contributed to another big victory over England, the fifth in succession.

Yet again, however, the Welsh fell behind early on, this time to a dropped goal which Cowan struck well into a strong wind. The reply came from John Bevan, by now a most consistent scorer, who crossed for an unconverted try. Soon Warfield had

to leave the field with concussion, and before England could send on Geoff Evans as a replacement Wales had moved further ahead, Bennett placing a long diagonal punt expertly for Gerald Davies to gather and score another unconverted try. A third one fell to Gareth Edwards after Sam Doble had placed a penalty for England, but at 12–6 the match seemed far from won as the home team turned to face the wind.

John Taylor was at last successful for Wales with a place kick, but his penalty was cancelled out by

another from Doble and the score remained at 15–9 until a remarkable period of time added on for injury in which the gap between the teams leaped by ten points. First came a try for skipper Arthur Lewis as a result of the move called after him — the 'Arthur'.

GARETH EDWARDS: Given a big, powerful centre like Arthur Lewis, this was a very effective ploy carried out near our opponents' goal-line. My role was to run flat from a set scrum with the ball, to draw the opposing halves and back row men towards the midfield. Phil Bennett helped by keeping station just outside me. Then I flipped the ball to Arthur, whose aim was to cut back at an angle towards the line — hopefully with enough momentum to cross it. But even if a try didn't result we would be in a good position to exploit second-phase possession.

On this occasion Arthur made slicing his way to the line look easy. But no one should be misled — the move called for great courage and commitment.

Phil Bennett kicked a simple conversion, and there was still enough time before no-side for Wales to provide the best sequence of combined play the game had offered. All the Welsh back division handled, and once more John Bevan was the man who crossed the line. His try remained unconverted, but yet again Wales had shown the staying-power which enabled them to play much of their best rugby during the final quarter of a match.

3 February 1973 at Murrayfield
SCOTLAND 10 (1G 1T)
WALES 9 (3PG)

the momentum achieved a fortnight earlier in Cardiff. McHarg and Brown dominated the lines-out and the Scots front row even managed to unsettle the Welsh at the set scrummages where the visitors usually reigned supreme.

MERVYN DAVIES: Ian McLauchlan — 'Mighty Mouse' — was captaining Scotland, and presumably it was he who dreamed up the notorious crabbing manœuvre which made it almost impossible for us to win crisp, clean possession on our put-in. The scrummages were never stable enough.

GARETH EDWARDS: I tried to delay feeding the scrum until it was steady. But like all French referees, M. Palmade wanted the game to keep flowing and directed me to get the ball in fast, threatening to penalize me if I disobeyed.

FACT BOX

J. P. R. Williams became Wales's most-capped post-War full back, overtaking Terry Davies (21 appearances).

Scotland A. R. Irvine, W. C. C. Steele, I. R. McGeechan, I. W. Forsyth, D. Shedden, C. M. Telfer, D. W. Morgan, A. B. Carmichael, R. L. Clark, J. McLauchlan (Captain). A. F. McHarg, P. C. Brown, N. A. MacEwan, G. M. Strachan, J. G. Millican.

Wales J. P. R. Williams (L. Welsh), T. G. R. Davies (L. Welsh), R. T. E. Bergiers, (Lanelli), A. J. Lewis (Ebbw Vale, Captain), J. C. Bevan (Cardiff), P. Bennett (Llanelli), G. O. Edwards (Cardiff), D. J. Lloyd (Bridgend), J. Young (L. Welsh), G. Shaw (Neath), W. D. Thomas (Llanelli), D. L. Quinnell (Llanelli), W. D. Morris (Neath), T. M. Davies (Swansea), J. Taylor (L. Welsh).

SCORERS
Scotland *Tries* — Telfer, Steele; *Con.* — Morgan.
Wales *Pens.* — Bennett (2), Taylor.

Referee: F. Palmade (FRF).

After nine matches without defeat in the Five Nations' Championship Wales's wings were clipped in Edinburgh, where Scotland won the fixture for the first time since 1967.

GARETH EDWARDS: In the Championship, England are the team Wales most want to beat and against whom we make our big effort. There's always the danger of a reaction after a good performance against them. That was what happened this year against the Scots — not for the first time!

The key period in the game was the opening quarter, when Scotland threw everything into an effort to prevent an unchanged Welsh XV from recovering

Welsh defenders are wide-eyed and legless as Billy Steele angles back for a try to give Scotland their decisive ten-point lead.

MERVYN DAVIES: Scotland's view seemed to be, 'If we can't win tidy possession then the other side is not going to either.' The crabbing infuriated me, since it was negative and ugly. But it certainly helped to unsettle Wales.

After eight minutes' play sustained pressure caused John Williams to carry over his own line, conceding a five-yard scrummage. The strike by Scottish hooker Clark was clean, and Douglas Morgan sent Colin Telfer speeding towards the Welsh posts. Fatally, the defending centres stayed on their own men, while Telfer, instead of passing to Forsyth or McGeechan, accelerated through the gap which had opened up and crossed the line for just the start his side had wanted. The conversion was kicked by Douglas Morgan.

After twenty minutes a tremendous run by Andy Irvine, supported by McEwan, again forced Wales to concede a five-yard scrummage. This time Telfer was a decoy-runner who drew away the opposing back row and allowed Billy Steele to dart in and accept Morgan's pass from the base of the scrum. A series of side-steps took him past Bennett and Mervyn Davies and over the line, just beyond the despairing grasp of John Williams. The clever try remained unconverted.

Bennett and Taylor kicked penalties for Wales before half-time, at which juncture Scotland led 10–6. To the great sides of earlier seasons a four-point deficit had seldom proved an insuperable obstacle, but the team of 1973 found itself lacking the inspiration to crack stout-hearted Scots resistance. All that could be managed in the remaining forty minutes was a Bennett penalty shortly before no-side.

GARETH EDWARDS: After this game I realized that Wales faced a long period of rebuilding.

We were going through a period of experiment, and caps were being awarded to some men who looked good in club fixtures but whose shortcomings were exposed at the very highest level.

World-beating teams do not develop overnight.

10 March 1973 at Cardiff
WALES   16 (1G 1T 2PG)
IRELAND   12 (1G 2PG)

Mike Gibson ringed by determined Welsh defenders. Before the final whistle, however, the Irish star got through for a clever try.

FACT BOX

In this 75th meeting between Wales and Ireland Gareth Edwards won his 30th cap — and became Cardiff's most-capped player: hitherto that distinction had belonged to Cliff Morgan (29 appearances).
The scrum half also lifted his tally of international points to 50 with a 12th try which enabled him to nose ahead of Gerald Davies (11).

Wales   J. P. R. Williams (L. Welsh), T. G. R. Davies (L. Welsh), R. T. E. Bergiers (Llanelli), A. J. Lewis (Ebbw Vale, Captain), J. L. Shanklin (L. Welsh), P. Bennett (Llanelli), G. O. Edwards (Cardiff), P. D. Llewelyn (Swansea), J. Young (L. Welsh), G. Shaw (Neath), W. D. Thomas (Llanelli), M. G. Roberts (L. Welsh), W. D. Morris (Neath), T. M. Davies (Swansea), J. Taylor (L. Welsh).

Ireland   A. H. Ensor, T. O. Grace, R. A. Milliken, C. M. H. Gibson, A. W. McMaster, B. J. McGann, J. J. Moloney, R. J. McLoughlin, K. W. Kennedy, J. F. Lynch, K. M. A. Mays, W. J. McBride (Captain), J. F. Slattery, T. A. P. Moore, S. A. McKinney.

SCORERS
Wales   Tries – Shanklin, Edwards; Con. – Bennett; Pens. – Bennett (2).
Ireland   Try – Gibson; Con. – McGann; Pens. – McGann (2).

Referee: T. F. E. Grierson (SRU).

Taking the view that Murrayfield had been an isolated off-day, the Welsh selectors named the same team to meet Ireland, only for John Bevan, Derek Quinnell and John Lloyd to drop out with injuries. London Welshmen Jim Shanklin and Mike Roberts came in, along with Swansea prop Phil Llewellyn.

GARETH EDWARDS: This was a season when everything seemed in a state of flux. For the game against us

Ireland chose a new full-back in Tony Ensor — and that meant that the long career of Tom Kiernan had come to an end. Willie John McBride began a momentous stint as his country's skipper.

I too was under pressure and having to cope with change, for since Barry John's retirement people had watched closely to see if I could survive without him. People criticized my new partnership with Phil Bennett without pausing to think that Phil was poles apart from Barry in temperament and approach, and that I had a lot of adjusting to do. Moreover, while Barry and I had polished our work together with regular outings for Cardiff, Phil was a member of another club.

I felt sure we would put it all together eventually — but not overnight!

After being narrowly off target with his first penalty attempt Phil Bennett drew blood for Wales twenty-five minutes into the game. Ireland were penalized for trampling, and the stand-off half's kick went over from 50 yards' range. Soon the visiting

forwards were penalized again a few yards into their own half, where they succumbed to the temptation of addressing caustic remarks to Scots referee Grierson. The indiscipline cost a 10-yard forfeit, which allowed Bennett to claim three more points from 45 yards out. Shortly before half-time a couple of Welsh forwards were offside at a ruck, and Barry McGann kicked a penalty for the Irish.

A few minutes into the second half Bennett gathered a loose kick ahead deep within his own half, had a quick look around, and decided that the time to attack was ripe. Two sizzling side-steps took him past the first wave of opponents, after which Glyn Shaw took up the running and penetrated Ireland's half. Then John Taylor ran well to set up a ruck from which the ball was delivered briskly to Gareth Edwards. The scrum-half bounced and buffeted his way towards the corner flag where, finally outnumbered, he passed inside to Shanklin. The wing crossed for an unconverted try to round off a tip-top movement.

GARETH EDWARDS: The build-up to that try was almost as important as the four points we got. To me it proved that although great players had vanished from the scene the new generation of Welsh International players could still put together some of the brilliant rugby played by the 1971 team. Maybe it had only been for two minutes this time, but soon we might be able to sustain it for ten or even twenty minutes.

McGann kept Ireland in the hunt with another penalty goal, but soon a Welsh attack featuring Bennett and Arthur Lewis ended with Edwards looping around Gerald Davies for a try close to the corner flag which Bennett converted with a fine kick.

The Irish departed the arena with honour, however, thanks to a clever try by Mike Gibson. As the ball came back from a scrummage on the Welsh 25-yard line McGann ran infield as a decoy. Gibson came very strongly towards the blind side, took a good pass from John Moloney and just reached the line. McGann's conversion completed the scoring.

24 March 1973 at Parc des Princes
FRANCE 12 (1DG 3PG)
WALES 3 (1DG)

FACT BOX

John Taylor won his 26th and last cap in this game, Phil Bennett his tenth.

France J.-M. Aguirre, J.-F. Philiponneau, C. Badin, J. Maso, J. Cantoni, J-P. Romeu, M. Pebeyre, J. Iracabal, R. Benesis, J.-L. Azarete, E. Cester, W. Spanghero (Captain), J.-C. Skrela, O. Saisset, J.-P. Biemouret.

Wales J. P. R. Williams (L. Welsh), T. G. R. Davies (L. Welsh), A. J. Lewis (Ebbw Vale), R. T. E. Bergiers (Llanelli), J. L. Shanklin (L. Welsh), P. Bennett (Llanelli), G. O. Edwards (Cardiff, Captain), P. D. Llewelyn (Swansea), J. Young (L. Welsh), G. Shaw (Neath), M. G. Roberts (L. Welsh), W. D. Thomas (Llanelli), J. Taylor (L. Welsh), T. M. Davies (Swansea), T. P. David (Llanelli).
Replacement: J. J. Williams (Llanelli) for Arthur Lewis.

SCORERS
France *Pens.* – Romeu (3); *D.G.* – Romeu.
Wales *Pen.* – Bennett.

Referee: D. P. d'Arcy (IRFU).

For their first visit to the magnificent new municipal stadium in Paris's south-western suburbs Wales had done some reshuffling. Gareth Edwards began another stint as skipper, but injuries to newly promoted men meant that in the end the team showed but one change. Dai Morris's absence from the scrummage back row after twenty-nine appearances allowed the awarding of a first cap to Tommy David, a stout-hearted flanker who had starred for Llanelli and the Barbarians in their victories over New Zealand.

However, his fiery presence could not inspire the visitors to produce any sort of form against a French XV which, after a Twickenham defeat, contained no fewer than ten newcomers. Each side registered a dropped goal, but whereas Wales's place-kicking was wayward Jean-Pierre Romeu put over three penalty goals out of four attempts.

PHIL BENNETT: Jean-Pierre was among the most prodigious kickers of my time. He first made an impression on me as a 16-year-old in a Youth International match at Llanelli when he elected to kick at goal from the ten-yard line inside his own half. I thought 'Cheeky so-and-so,' and positioned myself on the Welsh 25-line — only to gasp moments later as the ball whizzed above my head, still climbing as it cleared the crossbar! (Ironically, the score was disallowed because a French player had got in front of the ball.)

This day in Paris he was again spot-on, whereas my form was not good. My place-kicking method was to chip the ball towards the posts like a soccer player taking a corner kick, and the Gilbert ball used in Britain suited me perfectly. On the Continent they use a rounder ball with blunt ends which is better for long-range kickers who belt the ball hard, and never suited me.

Romeu's first points came two minutes into the game when Wales's line-out men were penalized for barging. From a range of close on 50 yards the ball fairly flew between the posts. Another gigantic effort — this time a drop-kick by Aguirre from the half-way line — missed narrowly before Romeu put over a simple penalty from 25 yards. The tall stand-off half dropped a goal before half-time after a French move which looked certain to produce a try was halted bravely by Arthur Lewis on the Welsh line. Hurt in the incident, the Ebbw Vale man left both the field and, as it turned out, International rugby.

PHIL BENNETT: Arthur's departure meant the folding of our tactical plan, which had been to submit the French midfield — and Jo Maso in particular — to the kind of intense pressure which we thought would make them crack. I must admit that it wasn't working even before Arthur left the field, for the French backs bravely tackled everything that moved.

Jim Shanklin moved into the centre, and wing John J. Williams came on for a first cap as a replacement. He proceeded to give a good account of himself in defence and attack, appearing unlucky at one stage not to be awarded a penalty try following a characteristic kick-and-chase foray into the French 25-yard area, where he was obstructed. From the resultant maul Phil Bennett put over a dropped goal.

Romeu clinched the match for France with another superb penalty, this time from 48 yards. Had Wales escaped defeat they would have been Champions, but as it was, each of the Five Nations won two and lost two of the games. The final table showed a unique quintuple tie.

A dropped goal and three penalties by Jean-Pierre Romeu were enough to defeat Wales, for whom Phil Bennett failed to strike form. In his first Championship season the French stand-off half contributed 26 of his country's 38 points.

MERVYN DAVIES: John Taylor and I found it strange without Dai Morris in this match. His great skill lay in ripping the ball from opponents' hands, so that John or I, arriving in support, could hand on possession to the backs.

John and Dai were not close friends off the field. In temperament and outlook they were poles apart. But they had enormous respect for each other's playing ability, which made their partnership a formidable one.

Championship Table 1972–73

Quintuple tie – teams in alphabetical order.

	P	W	D	L	PF	PA	Pts
ENGLAND (5)	4	2	0	2	52	62	4
FRANCE (4)	4	2	0	2	38	36	4
IRELAND (2)	4	2	0	2	50	48	4
SCOTLAND (2)	4	2	0	2	55	59	4
WALES (1)	4	2	0	2	53	43	4

Numbers in brackets indicate last season's positions in the unfinished Championship.

MATCH 35

10 November 1973 at Cardiff

WALES 24 (3T 4PG)
AUSTRALIA 0

A novel and highly entertaining visit by Japan occupied the early autumn in Wales, after which the Wallabies arrived for a more serious confrontation. Hit by the defection of leading players to the rival Rugby League code, Australia had suffered defeats the previous season at the hands of New Zealand, France and even Tonga, but still drew a capacity crowd to the Arms Park for the Test against Wales. *Waltzing Matilda* figured loudly in the musical repertoire.

The Welsh selectors had awarded first caps to Bobby Windsor of Pontypool RFC and Allan Martin of Aberavon.

MERVYN DAVIES: A great pair of recruits! Bobby may not have been the best hooker pure and simple with whom I played, but his sheer zest for the game was unrivalled. He could make quieter team-mates bristle with aggression.

This was useful with Allan, who was really a gentle giant. Great technical skill was his strong point, and he did amazingly well to keep his standard of line-out work so high at a period when scarcely any competitor for his International place emerged in Wales.

Dai Morris was also back to prove that he still had much to offer in a pack which held a five-stone advantage over the tourists. Thus Australia's forwards conceded a succession of first-half penalties as they strove to keep their opponents at bay. Phil Bennett was back in form as a place-kicker, putting four attempts over and hitting the posts twice.

It was J. P. R. Williams who spurred Wales to a very good second-half display which yielded three tries.

J. P. R. WILLIAMS: After half-time the situation was tailor-made for an attacking full-back. With the Australian pack well beaten, all the possession was coming our way and I could safely move up with our three-quarters as often as I wished. Soon I was able to give Gerald Davies a scoring pass down the blind side.

The other points-getters for Wales were Dai Morris, who crossed from a ruck just short of the Wallabies' line, and — on his debut — Bobby Windsor. Just before the close Clive Shell came on as a replacement for Gareth Edwards, touching the ball just once in the course of gaining his single cap for Wales.

GARETH EDWARDS: Tweaking a hamstring in the closing minutes was the last straw — for although our display showed up well on the scoreboard I was dissatisfied with it. Australia were a poor side, and we should have scored several more tries.

I am glad that Clive Shell had his replacement cap like 'Chico' Hopkins before him, for I am well aware that my long International career kept out a number of scrum-halves who might have played often for Wales in another era.

Probably it is slim comfort to players like Clive, 'Chico', Martyn Davies, Selwyn Williams and one or two others, but I must say that their presence on the Welsh scene certainly kept the man in possession on his toes.

Looking ahead to the Championship, it seemed that Wales's principal problems lay in the centre, where direction and cohesion had been missing since the retirement of John Dawes. Against Australia Keith Hughes and Roy Bergiers formed the first of four pairings used during the season.

Bobby Windsor *(right)* **pursues a loose ball. His sheer zest for the game was unrivalled, says Mervyn Davies.**

19 January 1974 at Cardiff

WALES 6 (1G)
SCOTLAND 0

FACT BOX

Gareth Edwards captained Wales for the tenth time.

Wales J. P. R. Williams (L. Welsh), T. G. R. Davies (L. Welsh), K. Hughes (L. Welsh), I. Hall (Aberavon), J. J. Williams (Llanelli), P. Bennett (Llanelli), G. O. Edwards (Cardiff, Captain), G. Shaw (Neath), R. W. Windsor (Pontypool), P. D. Llewelyn (Swansea), A. J. Martin (Aberavon), D. L. Quinnell (Llanelli), W. D. Morris (Neath), T. M. Davies (Swansea), T. J. Cobner (Pontypool).

Scotland A. R. Irvine, A. D. Gill, J. M. Renwick, I. R. McGeechan, L. G. Dick, C. M. Telfer, A. J. M. Lawson, J. McLauchlan (Captain), D. F. Madsen, A. B. Carmichael, A. F. McHarg, G. L. Brown, W. Lauder, W. S. Watson, N. A. MacEwan.

SCORERS
Wales *Try* – Cobner; *Con.* – Bennett.

Referee: R. F. Johnson (RFU).

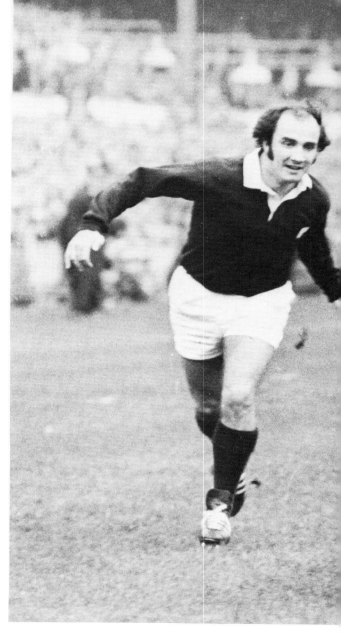

This was the hundredth International match to be staged at Cardiff Arms Park, but sadly Wales and Scotland could not produce a game worthy of the occasion. One of few players to enjoy it to the full was Terry Cobner, the Pontypool RFC flanker, who marked his first International appearance with a try.

There appeared to be a lack of *hwyl* and commitment about the Welsh XV, and twenty-three minutes went by before they managed to produce a purposeful move. To the faint surprise of 50,000 onlookers, it brought them the lead.

GERALD DAVIES: I had been feeling frustrated at not getting into the game when suddenly Phil Bennett came weaving towards my wing and gave me the ball with a bit of room to move. A change of pace and a side-step or two took me past Andy Irvine and Nairn MacEwan before a third

coverer brought me down. Terry Cobner did marvellously to be in such close support and thoroughly deserved the try he scored after taking my pass.

Some Scottish players thought that I should have been penalized for playing the ball after a tackle, claiming that the ball touched the ground. It did not. I protected it from the turf and bobbed it up to Terry all in one movement.

Phil Bennett goaled the try, but Scotland were by no means downhearted to be a mere 6–0 down at the interval with the benefit of the breeze to come. They now launched an offensive which brought the very best out of the Welsh defenders.

MERVYN DAVIES: I much preferred tackling to try-scoring, so I enjoyed myself a lot as the Scots turned on the pressure. Colin Telfer, Ian McGeechan and Jim Renwick all had to be picked off as they went for gaps in our midfield.

J.P.R. and Gerald, too, saved tries with great cover tackles.

However, it was not all Scotland, and before the close Mervyn Davies got across the visitors' line only to lose his grip on the ball. Afterwards supporters' tongues wagged over the team's low-key showing.

A debut try coming up for a Welsh flank forward: Terry Cobner about to take a pass from Gerald Davies and score.

GARETH EDWARDS: A lot of people were dissatisfied, not thoroughly understanding the rebuilding that was still being done. In the great years at the beginning of the decade Welsh supporters had got used to regular helpings of success. Now it was patience they needed, while the players and the selectors sought to get things right.

2 February 1974 in Dublin

IRELAND 9 (3PG)
WALES 9 (1G 1PG)

FACT BOX

Wales were the first side in 15 matches and two years to escape defeat when playing away from home.
Phil Bennett's five points took his personal tally for Wales to 50.

Ireland A. H. Ensor, V. A. Becker, C. M. H. Gibson, R. A. Milliken, P. Lavery, M. A. M. Quinn, J. J. Moloney, J. F. Lynch, K. W. Kennedy, R. J. McLoughlin, W. J. McBride (Captain), M. I. Keane, J. F. Slattery, T. A. P. Moore, S. M. Deering.

Wales J. P. R. Williams (L. Welsh), C. F. W. Rees (L. Welsh), I. Hall (Aberavon), A. A. J. Finlayson (Cardiff), J. J. Williams (Llanelli), P. Bennett (Llanelli), G. O. Edwards (Cardiff, Captain), G. Shaw (Neath), R. W. Windsor (Pontypool), W. P. J. Williams (Neath), G. A. D. Wheel (Swansea), A. J. Martin (Aberavon), W. D. Morris (Neath), T. M. Davies (Swansea), T. J. Cobner (Pontypool).

SCORERS
Ireland *Pens.* – Ensor (3).
Wales *Try* – J. J. Williams; *Con.* – Bennett; *Pen.* – Bennett.

Referee: K. A. Pattinson (RFU).

After their showing against Scotland the odds seemed stacked against Wales, last victorious in Dublin ten years earlier. Victories were going to teams playing at home, none of the Five Nations having won an away match for some time. Further, the visitors were fielding four new caps in Geoff Wheel of Swansea RFC, Walter Williams, a Neath RFC prop, Alex Finlayson of Cardiff at centre, and Clive Rees, a product of Loughborough College who was now a wing with London Welsh. He had the difficult task of standing in for an unavailable Gerald Davies, and like the others, seemed more of a stop-gap choice than an investment for the future.

Ireland took first use of a gusting wind, which interfered with the players' best intentions. Little, however, went right for the home team's place-kickers. Tony Ensor put over two penalties before half-time, but also missed with three attempts. Quinn was also wide twice, so that the interval arrived with the score tied 6–6, Wales having contrived a try by J. J. Williams, converted.

J. P. R. WILLIAMS: Curiously it came from poor-quality possession, at a scrum near Ireland's line on the Welsh left. Dai Morris tidied up our heel and heard Phil Bennett call for the ball on the blind side, having noted that the Irish back row had all gone tearing off towards our midfield. I supported Phil and quickly tossed a longish pass to J.J. who took it in his stride and went in for the try.

It was a good score, owing much to quick thinking and opportunism, and also simple in the end — which is strange, because at Lansdowne Road you usually had no time to think before being gunned down by Irish tacklers!

GARETH EDWARDS: Phil Bennett put over a magnificent conversion, and I was delighted that we reached half-time all square. There seemed no way the Irish could hold us against the breeze.

The refereeing of Ken Pattinson, however, now turned the game into a stalemate and effectively prevented Wales from pressing home our advantage. We used the wind to gain ground and reach the opposing 25-area — only for the referee to penalize our forwards again and again at the line-out, and allow Ireland to keep us out of attacking range.

That evening we had it out. Ken said that since he could see Welsh infringements he had no alternative but to award penalties. I accused him of positioning himself continually on our side of the line-out, thus being unable to see the tricks Ireland were getting up to.

Willie John McBride refrained from an official comment — but the gleam never left his eye through the whole of the second half!

Tony Ensor put Ireland into the lead with his first place-kick of the second half, and not until much later did Phil Bennett achieve the 35-yard penalty which gave his side a draw. A rather unexpected result, it looked capable of helping Wales along the road to a Championship title.

As it turned out, of course, the season's honours were to go to the Irish. The point they got on the day was to put them on top of the Five Nations table for the first time since 1949.

Allan Martin contests possession for Wales. But the season's honours went to Ireland.

16 February 1974 at Cardiff

WALES 16 (1T 1DG 3PG)
FRANCE 16 (1T 1DG 3PG)

FACT BOX

Wales J. P. R. Williams (L. Welsh),
T. G. R. Davies (L. Welsh), I. Hall (Aberavon),
A. A. J. Finlayson (Cardiff), J. J. Williams
(Llanelli), P. Bennett (Llanelli), G. O. Edwards
(Cardiff, Captain), G. Shaw (Neath),
R. W. Windsor (Pontypool), W. P. J. Williams
(Neath), I. R. Robinson (Cardiff), D. L. Quinnell
(Llanelli), W. D. Morris (Neath), T. M. Davies
(Swansea), T. J. Cobner (Pontypool).

France J-M. Aguirre, R. Bertranne, J. Pecune,
J-P. Lux, A. Dubertrand, J-P. Romeu,
J. Fouroux, J. Iracabal, R. Benesis, A. Vaquerin,
E. Cester (Captain), A. Esteve, J-C. Skrela,
C. Spanghero, V. Boffelli.

SCORERS
Wales *Try* – J. J. Williams;
Pens. – Bennett (3); *D.G.* – Edwards.
France *Try* – Lux; *Pens.* – Romeu (3);
D.G. – Romeu.

Referee: N. R. Sanson (SRU).

Wales's only try, scored by J. J. Williams who took advantage of a slender chance in brilliant fashion.

GARETH EDWARDS: The score-line looks thrilling, with two sides sharing 32 points. But in reality this was another unsatisfactory game. Most of the excitement seemed to happen off the field. For example, the rest of the team understood that Phil Bennett had cried off with 'flu and was to be replaced by understudy John Bevan of Aberavon — John certainly thought so on Saturday morning and was looking forward enormously to his first cap. Then we heard that Phil had declared himself fit after all, and John would not be needed. I suspect that a couple of the selectors got their lines crossed.

In the end the day belonged to a third stand-off half, Jean-Pierre Romeu, who had been restored to France's team after a short absence. He put over three penalty goals as well as the last-second dropped goal which earned his country a draw. Despite their avoidance of defeat, however, the visiting XV were not judged by observers to be among their country's best sides.

Their plans had been laid soundly, and the monotonous efficiency with which Romeu put boot to ball kept Wales out of striking distance for much of the game. But there was no Gallic sparkle, and the try which gave them the lead after four minutes ought to have been prevented by the Welsh backs. France scrummaged hard on their opponents' 25-yard line, where Romeu for once fed Lux. Little Pecune's decoy run deceived the defending centres, and Lux, winning his 36th cap, dashed in unopposed for a try. Surprisingly, Romeu failed to kick the relatively straightforward conversion.

The other two memorable moments of the first half belonged to Wales. J. J. Williams took advantage of a slender chance in brilliant fashion after appearing to be cut off close to the North Stand

touch-line. Deftly chipping ahead, however, he showed expert ball control on France's goal-line, dribbling across for a superb unconverted try.

Then there was the Gareth Edwards dropped goal: on the retreat some 30 yards from the French posts he made as if to serve Bennett, changed his mind, and fired the ball like a mortar bomb high above the crossbar. A touch of genius.

GARETH EDWARDS: It was our coach at Cardiff Training College Roy Bish (later coach to Cardiff RFC) who used to say that a dropped goal was the easiest three points' worth in the book. I agree — whenever I put one over I felt as if I'd had something for nothing! Mind you, I missed a few too — and that's when the crowd really gives you stick!

Sometimes I deliberately looked for a chance to drop at goal, to vary our tactics and take pressure off the midfield. But on other occasions, like this one against France, I had no time to think, and just let fly. Those were the ones I enjoyed.

Bennett and Romeu now exchanged penalty goals, so that half-time arrived with the score 13–13. The second period saw continued good form by the Welsh forwards, particularly at the lines-out where new cap Ian Robinson's support for Derek Quinnell and Mervyn Davies contributed to a final count of 27 clean takes to 17. But well though Edwards and Bennett played, with Gerald Davies and J. J. Williams radiating menace on the wings, the midfield never looked smart enough to outwit their hard-tackling opposite numbers.

With nine minutes left a third penalty by Bennett seemed to have made the game safe for Wales. But as injury-time arrived France won a line-out on their opponents' 25-line, and Romeu's drop kick at goal was high and straight.

GARETH EDWARDS: I tried to reach Romeu and put pressure on him, but he was just too quick for me. The final whistle went — after which I don't think the French fans stopped singing and blowing bugles all evening!

I felt bitterly disappointed, as I thought we had done just enough to deserve victory. This draw, following the one in Ireland, seemed to have robbed the season of all challenge and incentive.

MATCH 39

16 March 1974 at Twickenham

ENGLAND 16 (1G 1T 2PG)
WALES 12 (1G 2PG)

Injury forced J. P. R. Williams to miss the last match of the Championship season, thus breaking a sequence of caps awarded since 1969. England's melancholy record against the visitors stretched back even further: they had not beaten Wales at Twickenham since 1960, and not at all for eleven years. On this day they stemmed the tide.

Not, however, without heated recriminations. Attending his last match as Wales's coach, Clive Rowlands was angered by refereeing decisions from Ireland's John West which certainly cost the visitors a draw if not victory. One of these came when Phil Bennett broke past the England defence and headed for the goal-line with unmarked players on his right. The referee chose this moment to blow for obstruction — and award a penalty to Wales.

PHIL BENNETT: It was a bad decision. Expecting Alan Old to tackle me, England's backs came up very fast, so that when I got round Old there were three team-mates with me and only full-back Dusty Hare to beat. That was when the whistle went, robbing Wales of a legitimate — and very large — advantage. Instead of a straightforward conversion to take, I found myself lining up a penalty kick at goal to try and salvage three points from a situation where we could have had six.

Another error — in the eyes of many onlookers — occurred late in the game, with Wales struggling hard to get on terms. J. J. Williams scorched away down the left wing, and characteristically chipped ahead over England's line. Showing the speed of a crack sprinter, he narrowly won the race to touch down against desperate coverers David Duckham and Peter Squires. This time apparently unsighted, Mr West blew for a 25-yard drop out.

During the first half little had happened to suggest that England were in with a chance of victory, Mervyn Davies having collected an opening try for their opponents.

MERVYN DAVIES: Dai Morris hacked a loose ball from the rear of an England line-out across the goal line — and you can imagine the satisfaction it gave me to produce a sprint that beat the challenge of defender Dave Duckham! Some people said I must have been offside, but the referee didn't think so, and that's good enough for me.

For the second time, however, a defensive lapse had allowed me to score against England. Had I been their captain that day I would have given them one helluva roasting. Near the goal-line, defence must be completely watertight and disciplined. Sloppiness cannot be tolerated.

Phil Bennett converted, and added a penalty goal to the tally, England's points coming from an Old penalty goal and a cracking try by David Duckham.

J. P. R. WILLIAMS: As a spectator at the game I gave high marks to my deputy, Roger Blyth of Swansea RFC, to whom I had sent a good luck telegram beforehand. However, if I had been at full-back 'Duckers' might not have scored his try.

Knowing his play, I would have guarded against the left-footed side-step which took him past Roger Blyth. It was always vital to deprive Dave of that option and force him to use his weaker foot.

England moved into the lead, however, through an individual effort by number 8 Andy Ripley. At a scrummage near the Welsh line he picked up and swept past leaden-footed back-row defenders for a try Old converted. The stand-off increased his side's winning margin with a second penalty goal, to which Bennett replied after the obstruction ruling described above.

Afterwards the visitors' dissatisfaction at aspects of the match was tempered by the manifest delight of England. They had laid a bogy which had haunted them for more than a decade.

A third talking-point which bore on the refereeing of the match emerged subsequently when video-tape recordings were being studied.

As Andy Ripley went around the scrummage from the number 8 position on his way to scoring England's second try he inadvertently put a hand on the back of a flanker in front of him. Although he gained no advantage, the letter of the law as it read at the time had been broken, and an 'accidental offside' ruling would have been in order. But it was a difficult infringement to spot, and possibly as a result of the incident the law was amended.

Championship Table 1973–74

	P	W	D	L	PF	PA	Pts
IRELAND	4	2	1	1	50	45	5
SCOTLAND	4	2	0	2	41	35	4
WALES	4	1	2	1	43	41	4
FRANCE	4	1	2	1	43	53	4
ENGLAND	4	1	1	2	63	66	3

Mervyn Davies exploits a defensive error by England to outpace the defence and score the visitors' only try.

Last season ended in a five-way tie.

18 January 1975 at Parc des Princes
FRANCE 10 (1T 2PG)
WALES 25 (1G 4T 1PG)

FACT BOX

On his 30th appearance for Wales Mervyn Davies assumed the captaincy of his country.

France M. Taffary, J-F. Gourdon, C. Dourthe, R. Bertranne, J-P. Lux, J-P. Romeu, J. Fouroux (Captain), A. Vaquerin, A. Paco, J-L. Azarete, G. Senal, A. Esteve, V. Boffelli, J-P. Bastiat, O. Saisset. *Replacements:* J. Cantoni for Gourdon, J-C. Skrela for Saisset.

Wales J. P. R. Williams (L. Welsh), T. G. R. Davies (Cardiff), R. W. R. Gravell (Llanelli), S. P. Fenwick (Bridgend), J. J. Williams (Llanelli), J. D. Bevan (Aberavon), G. O. Edwards (Cardiff), A. G. Faulkner (Pontypool), R. W. Windsor (Pontypool), G. Price (Pontypool), A. J. Martin (Aberavon), G. A. D. Wheel (Swansea), T. J. Cobner (Pontypool), T. M. Davies (Swansea, Captain), T. P. Evans (Swansea).

SCORERS
France *Try* – Gourdon; *Pens.* – Taffary (2).
Wales *Tries* – Fenwick, Cobner, Gerald Davies, Edwards, Price; *Con.* – Fenwick; *Pen.* – Fenwick.

Referee: K. A. Pattinson (RFU).

At the beginning of the 1974–75 season, in line with broader changes then taking place in Britain, the dimensions of the game became metric. In practice this had no effect on the character of the play, though henceforth reference would be made, for instance, to the 'twenty-two-metre line' instead of the 'twenty-five-yard line' and so on.

For France this was a catastrophic day. At the hands of a new-look Wales, the Tricolours went down to their heaviest home defeat since the Springboks' visit of 1952.

No fewer than six new caps took the field for the visitors, including John Bevan of Aberavon in place of an off-form Phil Bennett who had not recovered from his demanding tour of South Africa the previous summer. John Dawes had succeeded Clive Rowlands as national team coach, and persuaded his fellow-selectors to nominate Mervyn Davies as captain.

GARETH EDWARDS: Although disappointed to lose the captaincy — again! — I had expected a change. Our new coach and his chosen skipper enjoyed a special relationship dating back to their London Welsh days together. I lost no time in assuring 'Swerve' that he could count on a hundred per cent effort from me.

MERVYN DAVIES: I was grateful for that backing. This was a pressure game for me, leading my country for the first time at Parc des Princes of all places. In another sense, though, the team and I had nothing to lose, for we had been written off before the match even began.

Critics had a lot of words to eat as the rejunevated Welsh XV gained (and surrendered) a fortuitous lead early on before applying itself methodically and relentlessly to grinding down French resistance.

The game was only three minutes old when an abortive drop at goal by Gareth Edwards bounced awkwardly for Lux, allowing Steve Fenwick to snap up an unconverted try.

GARETH EDWARDS: My miscued kick was a blessing in disguise. It allowed Steve, on his debut, to make an early impact. After that he had no trouble settling down.

A Fenwick penalty also put Wales level after France had nosed ahead through Gourdon's try and a penalty by Taffary, and with John Bevan marshalling the backs like a veteran, the visitors soon swept back into the lead. The ball was spun sweetly to the right, where a half-break by Ray Gravell was followed by an early pass to Gerald Davies. The wing danced infield to feed the perfectly positioned Mervyn Davies, who put Cobner in for a try which Fenwick converted. Soon Gerald Davies was again in action, this time showing expert control with the feet and steering a loose ball across the French line for a score which remained unconverted.

Throughout the second half France's supporters booed and hooted their team, especially when Gareth Edwards sped past a slow-witted defence for a fourth Welsh try. Fouroux's men did their best to respond, but a series of desperate attacks was rewarded only by a second Taffary penalty. Wales not only held on but also had the stamina to strike a final blow. Prop Graham Price booted a loose ball out of the Welsh 22-area, J. J. Williams raced like a greyhound across to the right and harassed Lux into a handling error, and again it was Price who arrived to trundle ten final metres for a try.

'Up and Under, Here We Go!' – shortly to be immortalised in verse by Max Boyce, the Pontypool front row forms up for the first time in the scarlet of Wales. From left, Graham Price, Bobby Windsor and Charlie Faulkner.

MERVYN DAVIES: The only word for it is sensational! Having tackled an opponent just before Graham broke away I could not give close support — so I enjoyed the luxury of standing at the half-way line, hands on hips, and seeing him romp into the distance and over our opponents' line.

I was pleased at the way our newcomers had fitted in with established players. After some mediocre seasons, there could be good days ahead for Wales!

Price's try remained unconverted, but no matter: Wales had achieved their biggest winning margin in Paris since 1911.

GARETH EDWARDS: This was a memorable and very important match, in which Wales rediscovered style and authority. I believe there were several good reasons for our success.

One – John Dawes's unworried approach to the game. 'You may not be a very good side today,' he told us beforehand. 'But by the end of the season you will be, I promise.'

Two – the arrival of Charlie Faulkner and Graham Price to join Bobby Windsor and complete the legendary Pontypool front row. As individuals they were formidable — as a trio they were the greatest! I can vouch for that, and few people saw them in action from closer than myself!

Three – into the team came that Superpatriot, Ray Gravell. Whether singing Welsh folk-songs to soothe his nerves or jabbing team-mates on the chest and demanding how they thought he would play, 'Grav' could be relied upon to banish hypertension from any changing-room!

BARRY JOHN: I agree with Gareth, and would add another reason — John Bevan's play at stand-off half. Here was a player who ran straight, taking the play to the opposing back row and committing it.

His International career, blighted by injury, was all too short.

MATCH 41

15 February 1975 at Cardiff

WALES 20 (1G 2T 2PG)
ENGLAND 4 (1T)

As with the previous five encounters between Wales
and England at Cardiff, the result of this game was
never in doubt. Opening ferociously, the home side
had built a winning lead of 16–0 by half-time, after
which they were surprisingly held in check by an
England combination which played much good
rugby.

The selectors retained the XV which had done so
well in Paris, and again there were many plus-factors

on which to reflect after the final whistle. Allan
Martin enjoyed his best Championship game as a
place-kicker for Wales, reproducing the form he had
shown the previous winter in setting an Aberavon
club record of 285 points for the season. England's
halves Webster and Cooper were ruthlessly harassed
by Trevor Evans and Terry Cobner, a pair of
flankers worthy to succeed Dai Morris and John
Taylor.

MERVYN DAVIES: As the third member of the back
row, I could change to a style of play I preferred. With the
previous pair I would hang back in the wake of their
sorties, to tidy up any mistakes that were made.

Trevor, an 80-minute player, and 'Cob', a fearsome
tackler for a man of his stature, preferred to exert pressure
close to the scrum on the opposing halves. So I was able to
stretch my legs a bit and move out to give support to our
midfield players.

Martin claimed the first points with a 50-metre
penalty, after which the backs hit their stride. An
electrifying scissors move between John Bevan and
Ray Gravell was borne on by Steve Fenwick, who
gave a scoring pass to J. J. Williams. Although the
conversion attempt fell short, Martin soon put over
another penalty, from 40 metres' range.

Sternly led by Mervyn Davies, the forwards were
carrying the battle to the English, mauling skilfully
and slewing the visiting scrummage round when
close to touch to neutralize their possession. The
backs, much encouraged, brought off another fine
move just before the interval, this time on the right.

J. P. R. WILLIAMS: Ray Gravell made a short burst on
the blind side a short distance from England's line and
passed to me. He had drawn a couple of defenders, and the
wing had to come infield to tackle me. My quick pass over
his head found Gerald Davies, who scored. I cannot claim
to have seen 'Reames', as we called him, but he was such a
great wing that I expected him to be there — and he was!

By this time a number of us had played together so often
that we released the ball without a qualm, confident that
support would be at hand. Mervyn Davies himself, with
those long arms and huge hands, was always among the
closest!

Martin completed the first-half scoring by firing his
conversion precisely between the posts.

Around the middle period of the game casualties
were suffered by both sides, Webster and Wheeler
of England and Wheel of Wales being replaced by
Steve Smith, John Pullin and Derek Quinnell. And
after the interval the visitors more than held their
own. Cooper at last managed to shake off the Welsh
back row and send his centres off on threatening
forays, in which Tony Jorden frequently joined
from full-back. To the crowd's disappointment

Sparkling work by the Welsh midfield players put J. J. Williams clear to run in the first Welsh try.

Wales settled for containment, and idled their way along until ten minutes from time, when at a line-out they conceded a try to Nigel Horton. Stung to action, Merv the Swerve and his men staged a grandstand finish with a try by Steve Fenwick that capped dazzling inter-passing.

The victory was satisfactory, but critics wondered why the Welsh had not sustained their pressure and picked up the extra 12 or 15 points which had seemed within their reach at half-time.

MERVYN DAVIES: So did I! Sure, England raised their game in the second half, but we should have been ready for them. In boxing parlance, we had let out opponents get up off the floor after delivering what should have been knock-out punches.

MATCH 42

1 March 1975 at Murrayfield

SCOTLAND 12 (1DG 3PG)
WALES 10 (1T 2PG)

FACT BOX

The Scottish authorities estimate that 105,000 people saw the game, a world record for a rugby match. Unofficial estimates put the figure as high as 120,000 — and certainly thousands more were unable to obtain entry to Murrayfield.

Scotland A. R. Irvine, W. C. C. Steele, J. M. Renwick, D. L. Bell, L. G. Dick, I. R. McGeechan, D. W. Morgan, J. McLauchlan (Captain), D. F. Madsen, A. B. Carmichael, A. F. McHarg, G. L. Brown, M. A. Biggar, D. G. Leslie, N. A MacEwan.

Wales J. P. R. Williams (L. Welsh), T. G. R. Davies (Cardiff), S. P. Fenwick (Bridgend), R. W. R. Gravell (Llanelli), J. J. Williams (Llanelli), J. D. Bevan (Aberavon), G. O. Edwards (Cardiff), A. G. Faulkner (Pontypool), R. W. Windsor (Pontypool), G. Price (Pontypool), M. G. Roberts (L. Welsh), A. J. Martin (Aberavon), T. J. Cobner (Pontypool), T. M. Davies (Swansea, Captain), T. P. Evans (Swansea).
Replacements: P. Bennett (Llanelli) for John Bevan; W. R. Blyth (Swansea) for Steve Fenwick.

SCORERS
Scotland *Pens.* – Morgan (3); *D.G.* – McGeechan.
Wales *Try* – Evans; *Pens.* – Fenwick (2).

Referee: J. R. West (IRFU).

Championship form lurched uncertainly from match to match this winter. France, taken apart by Wales, recovered to beat Scotland 10–9; and now, before a record crowd for British rugby of around 100,000, the new-look Welsh XV found Murrayfield's atmosphere just too much, even on St David's Day. Struggling for composure throughout (and affected by injuries to key men), they left their final rally until it was too late.

The game swings away from Wales: stand-off half John Bevan is helped from the field nursing a shoulder injury. Phil Bennett replaced him, and soon Steve Fenwick had to make way for Roger Blyth.

Mike Roberts, promoted to replace the injured Geoff Wheel, won one of his sporadic caps as Allan Martin's partner in an otherwise unchanged Welsh side. But fire to match Scotland's was never kindled within the visitors' ranks. Ian McLauchlan's pack won supremacy at the early scrummages, Gordon Brown and Alastair McHarg were in dominant form at the lines-out, and the resultant flow of possession was expertly used by Douglas Morgan at scrum-half. He did not move the ball a great deal, preferring to keep his rampaging forwards on the advance with a variety of tactical kicks. Three penalty goals by him from long range also provided match-winning points, Scotland's other score coming from an Ian McGeechan dropped goal.

The game, however, swung irredeemably away from Wales in the twenty-sixth minute. That was when John Bevan — acclaimed by critics for having brought zip and direction to the Welsh midfield in his first two International appearances — had to leave the field with an injured shoulder.

MERVYN DAVIES: Barely a minute after he had come on as replacement, I asked Phil Bennett to take a penalty kick at goal. He tried to refuse, saying that he had not properly warmed up, only for me to pull rank and insist. He missed.

I was left asking myself ruefully why I hadn't done the sensible thing and used Steve Fenwick or Allan Martin. The mistake was one of several reminders in this match that as a captain I had a great deal still to learn.

Perhaps unsettled by this incident, Phil Bennett could produce only a low-key peformance. Another serious blow to the visitors was the loss of Steve Fenwick, whose two penalties had kept his side in the hunt, with a fractured cheek-bone. Roger Blyth of Swansea RFC, a full-back, took his place in the centre.

So Wales muddled their way along without threatening to disturb Scotland's grip on the game until the fourth minute of injury time.

GERALD DAVIES: At long last I got a pass with room to move in, and brought off two side-steps that took me into Scotland's 22-area. Trevor Evans did well to arrive in support, taking my pass and beating off two or three desperate Scotsmen to reach the corner flag.

His try only highlighted what we might have achieved by moving the ball earlier in the game and stretching our opponents. Our defeat showed that we were not yet a great side despite two convincing victories, and that some bad habits had come back from the triumphant British Lions tour the previous summer. There seemed to be an obsession with the creation of a forward platform. Gareth Edwards seemed to be enjoying the novelty of the rolling touch-kick which he had perfected, and overdid it. J.P.R. seemed more concerned to take on tacklers in a physical confrontation and set up rucks than to make space for other backs. In other words, both the team and a number of individuals were still indulging in experiments — which were not always paying off.

Allan Martin's conversion attempt (which might have tied the score) began well, only for the ball to veer away from the posts. As the relieved Scotsmen caught it, Mr West blew the final whistle.

MERVYN DAVIES: Inexcusable penalties conceded by experienced, highly-skilled players had cost us this game. I spent the Edinburgh evening in a very gruff mood!

BARRY JOHN: I can understand 'Swerve's' displeasure! But in conceding two line-out penalties, it was clear from the Press box that Allan Martin had 'jumped across' in each case to compete for a throw-in that was not straight.

Rather than penalize him, the referee should have blown for a scrum or another line-out — that is, the first infringement.

Scotsmen Mike Biggar (7) and Billy Steele (14) bar the path of Wales flanker Trevor Evans (right). **In injury time the Swansea man forced his way across the line for a try which came too late.**

MATCH 43

15 March 1975 at Cardiff

WALES 32 (3G 2T 2PG)
IRELAND 4 (1T)

FACT BOX

Wales's 32 points made up their highest-ever score against Ireland; 32—4 was the biggest winning margin since 1907 (29—0) — and this was Ireland's heaviest defeat in the Championship since that match.
Gareth Edwards won his 40th cap.
With 14 tries in the season Wales could justify their position as Champions above their sole vanquishers Scotland, who gained just two tries.

Wales J. P. R. Williams (L. Welsh), T. G. R. Davies (Cardiff), R. W. R. Gravell (Llanelli), R. T. E. Bergiers (Llanelli), J. J. Williams (Llanelli), P. Bennett (Llanelli), G. O. Edwards (Cardiff), A. G. Faulkner (Pontypool), R. W. Windsor (Pontypool), G. Price (Pontypool), G. A. D. Wheel (Swansea), A. J. Martin (Aberavon), T. P. Evans (Swansea), T. M. Davies (Swansea, Captain), T. J. Cobner (Pontypool).

Ireland A. H. Ensor, T. O. Grace, R. A. Milliken, C. M. H. Gibson, A. W. McMaster, W. McCombe, J. J. Moloney, R. J. McLoughlin, K. W. Kennedy, R. J. Clegg, M. I. Keane, W. J. McBride (Captain), J. F. Slattery, W. P. Duggan, M. J. A. Sherry.

SCORERS
Wales *Tries* — Edwards, Gerald Davies, Faulkner, J. J. Williams, Bergiers; *Cons.* — Bennett (3); *Pens.* — Bennett (2).
Ireland *Try* — Duggan.

Referee: J. st Guilhem (FRF).

This was a day when the years finally caught up with Ireland's grizzled warriors. For an hour guile and brave defence kept even the most savage Welsh attacks at bay; but in the end, their vigour having been systematically sapped, the visitors cracked and conceded the biggest-ever points total for the fixture.

GARETH EDWARDS: Wales served up what I consider to have been the finest 20 minutes'-worth of rugby at Cardiff in a decade.

GERALD DAVIES: Mike Gibson told me afterwards that he had seldom felt so helpless during a match. 'There was nothing we could do to hold your team in that mood,' he admitted.

Adding to the home team's jubilation came news from Twickenham that an unfancied England team had beaten Scotland. The Five Nations' title was back in Wales.

The Welsh selectors had brought back a fit Geoff Wheel and covered the unavailability of Fenwick with Roy Bergiers. Phil Bennett was to continue at stand-off half while John Bevan nursed his injured shoulder — but could the Llanelli man produce some form after his indifferent game at Murrayfield?

PHIL BENNETT: This end-of-season game, on a sunny day in front of a relaxed, appreciative crowd, was just what the doctor ordered. I was not aware of any pressure — and that's the best frame of mind to be in, especially for a place-kicker. Witness my five successful shots at goal — and I hit the post twice too!

Bennett's enterprise also pleased spectators. Within ten minutes of the start he had moved the ball along his line, tested Irish full back Ensor with a towering up-and-under, and made a scampering blind-side break. It may be that the presence of three club colleagues in the back-line was encouraging him to cast aside dull care after his dismal winter.

The first Welsh try-scorer was Gareth Edwards, who broke three tackles and went in from 20 metres range.

GARETH EDWARDS: I felt one of those moments of exuberance with which most athletes and serious games-players will be familiar — just for a second or two it was like wearing seven-league boots and running faster than I had ever done before.

GERALD DAVIES: I was the next scorer, after a sustained spell of combined play which left all thirty players gasping for breath and the big crowd yelling itself hoarse! A scissors movement involving J.P.R. began it all, after which ruck followed ruck and we switched the ball in every kind of direction. I recall strong running from Roy Bergiers, and finally the ball came to the right for me to apply the coup de grâce. All tremendously exhilarating!

Next came a break by Bobby Windsor, whose pass five metres from the line sent in club-mate Charlie Faulkner for a first International try — capped by a memorable if toothless grin. J. J. Williams profited from a smartly won ruck and clever work by the half-backs to cross next, and finally the long-striding Roy Bergiers cruised over, brushing off tacklers

whose determination had long since evaporated.

It seemed as if the Irish were in for a whitewash, but near the end a cheeky reverse pass from Edwards did not go to hand. Willie Duggan intercepted and found the stamina to dash 30 metres to the line for an unconverted try.

GARETH EDWARDS: I could see the funny side of it, and laughed — much to the displeasure of a scowling J.P.R. 'We should have kept a clean sheet,' he told me angrily — and he meant it. What a competitor!

PHIL BENNETT: This was Willie John McBride's last game for Ireland. After one of our tries I caught sight of him on the Irish goal-line, hands on knees, head down, a picture of total exhaustion and dejection. I felt sad that so great a forward, who had led his Lions inspiringly in South Africa, should reach the end of the trail on such a bad day as this for his country.

Gerald Davies, Mike Slemen and Andy Irvine could scarcely have improved on the style: 'Charlie' Faulkner thunders in for Wales's fourth try against luckless Ireland.

Championship Table 1974–75

	P	W	D	L	PF	PA	Pts
WALES (2)	4	3	0	1	87	30	6
FRANCE (2)	4	2	0	2	53	79	4
IRELAND (1)	4	2	0	2	54	67	4
SCOTLAND (2)	4	2	0	2	47	40	4
ENGLAND (5)	4	1	0	3	40	65	2

Numbers in brackets indicate last season's positions.

103

MATCH 44

20 December 1975 at Cardiff

WALES   **28** (3G 1T 1DG 1PG)
AUSTRALIA   **3** (1PG)

FACT BOX

Wales registered a record win over Australia in a game when J. J. Williams scored only the second hat-trick of tries since the Second World War (Maurice Richards v. England, 1969, having obtained the first).

Wales   J. P. R. Williams (L. Welsh), J. J. Williams (Llanelli), R. W. R. Gravell (Llanelli), S. P. Fenwick (Bridgend), C. F. W. Rees (L. Welsh), J. D. Bevan (Aberavon), G. O. Edwards (Cardiff), A. G. Faulkner (Pontypool), R. W. Windsor (Pontypool), G. Price (Pontypool), A. J. Martin (Aberavon), G. A. D. Wheel (Swansea), T. J. Cobner (Pontypool), T. J. Davies (Swansea, Captain), T. P. Evans (Swansea).

Australia   P. E. McLean, P. G. Batch, R. D. L'Estrange, G. A. Shaw, L. E. Monaghan, J. C. Hindmarsh, J. N. B. Hipwell (Captain), J. E. C. Meadows, P. A. Horton, R. Graham, R. A. Smith, G. Fay, J. K. Lambie, G. Cornelson, A. A. Shaw.
Replacements: R. G. Hauser for John Hipwell; G. K. Pearse for John Lambie.

SCORERS
Wales   *Tries* – J. J. Williams (3), Edwards; *Cons.* – Fenwick (2), Martin; *Pen.* – Fenwick; *D.G.* – Bevan.
Australia   *Pen.* – McLean.

Referee: D. P. d'Arcy (IRFU).

stand-off half in place of Phil Bennett (foot injury) and Clive Rees in place of Gerald Davies (hamstring).

GERALD DAVIES: Clive was to be on the left, allowing J. J. Williams to appear on his favourite right wing, where he always turned out for Llanelli but where I usually played for Wales. He made a great job of adapting to the other wing for the National XV. But on this occasion, with myself unavailable, I knew he was looking forward to showing what he could do in his proper position. People had been saying, too, that he had lost some pace — so all in all I sat back to watch his display with some anticipation!

With Mervyn Davies in particularly good form Wales were able to dominate the lines-out, their final favourable ratio being 34–16 clean takes.

MERVYN DAVIES: Our battle plan was similar to the one we had used against Ireland in the spring. The Wallaby forwards had to be subdued first.

The plan worked, with Gareth Edwards playing his usual key role. The scrum-half's non-stop series of tactical kicks, many of them rolling and bouncing huge distances to touch, kept the opposition back-pedalling and broke their resolve to resist Wales's second-half offensive.

An azure sky, a perfect pitch, and a capacity crowd for Wales's last International match of the year, against an Australian side whose colours had been lowered several times on tour, but had also provided superb entertainment. A few days before the Test they ran up 51 points, including eight dazzling tries, against a Glamorgan XV.

Drafted into the Welsh XV were John Bevan at

GARETH EDWARDS: People congratulated me afterwards for the restraint and control I showed. Had they but known it, however, I was actually nursing a calf muscle whose fibres I had torn at training on the previous Thursday. But for hard work by our physiotherapist Gerry Lewis I might not have been able to take the field against the Wallabies.

The interesting thing about the slight handicap was that it prompted me to see if I could play a different sort of game from my usual full-blooded stop-at-nothing approach. Afterwards it was clear that I was capable of holding my instincts in check.

Torn fibres or not, Edwards could not resist following up Steve Fenwick's opening penalty by battling across the line from a scrummage to get Wales's first try. Fenwick's conversion meant that the home team led 9–3 at the interval, Paul McLean having kicked a penalty goal for the tourists.

Strained knee ligaments now forced John Hipwell from the field, Rod Hauser replacing him at scrum-half and the captaincy passing to Geoff Shaw. By this stage, flanker Gary Pearce was also on for the injured John Lambie.

The second half belonged to J. J. Williams. Excellent handling by the Welsh midfield sent the

Critics of J. J. Williams were saying before the game that he had lost the blistering pace of a season or so earlier. The Llanelli flier answered them with three tries like this against Australia.

sprinter in for two sizzling tries, after which he completed a hat-trick by doing his own thing. Chasing a beautifully weighted kick-ahead, he threaded his way through a clutch of defenders and won a thrilling race for the touch-down.

GERALD DAVIES: When the average rugby player strives for top speed you see his head rolling, his thighs pounding like pistons and his arms waving in all directions.

Watching J.J. from the stand, I reflected how effortlessly he moved. An International sprinter, and one of very few who have been able to make a mark in big rugby, he seemed to glide across the turf without wasting an ounce of energy.

Allan Martin and Steve Fenwick put over a conversion kick apiece, the other Welsh scorer being John Bevan with a dropped goal. Australia never gave up trying, but ploys and stratagems which had proved effective against provincial opponents posed no problems to a sound Welsh defence.

17 January 1976 at Twickenham
ENGLAND 9 (3PG)
WALES 21 (3G 1PG)

FACT BOX

Wales's 12-point winning margin was their highest-ever at Twickenham.
It was a great day for J. P. R. Williams:
- He scored the first pair of tries by a full back in international rugby.
- He broke Jack Bancroft's record of 33 caps for a Welsh full back.
- He had now scored on each of his three appearances at Twickenham.

Swansea RFC supplied a complete back row in the match. But whereas Mervyn Davies and Trevor Evans were with Wales, Mark Keyworth played for England!

England A. J. Hignell, P. J. Squires, A. Maxwell, D. Cooke, D. J. Duckham, M. J. Cooper, M. Lampkowski, F. E. Cotton, P. J. Wheeler, M. A. Burton, W. B. Beaumont, R. M. Wilkinson, M. Keyworth, A. G. Ripley, A. Neary (Captain),
Replacement: P. S. Preece for Squires.

Wales J. P. R. Williams (L. Welsh), T. G. R. Davies (Cardiff), R. W. R. Gravell (Llanelli), S. P. Fenwick (Bridgend), J. J. Williams (Llanelli), P. Bennett (Llanelli), G. O. Edwards (Cardiff), A. G. Faulkner (Pontypool), R. W. Windsor (Pontypool), G. Price (Pontypool), A. J. Martin (Aberavon), G. A. D. Wheel (Swansea), T. J. Cobner (Pontypool), T. M. Davies (Swansea, Captain), T. P. Evans (Swansea).

SCORERS
England *Pens.* – Hignell (3).
Wales *Tries* – J. P. R. Williams (2), Edwards; *Cons.* – Fenwick (3); *Pen.* – Martin.

Referee: G. Domercq (FRF).

Wales went into the Championship campaign with the confidence born of great strength in depth. Only seventeen players were to be used in the four matches, and the presence of battle-hardened men on the replacements' bench must have spurred the chosen élite to give consistently fine performances.

The preamble to this opening fixture, however, was less satisfactory. Picked as a stand-off half for the Trial match, Phil Bennett withdrew with a foot injury — only to turn out for Llanelli in a club game. The selectors' reaction was to name John Bevan as Gareth Edwards's partner, and promote 21-year-old David Richards to the job of understudy. Irony of ironies, both men were injured after being selected, and after all it was Bennett who took the field against England!

PHIL BENNETT: A niggling injury persuaded me to pull out of the Trial — a sub-representative match — though it was not bad enough to keep me out of my club XV, which was in the middle of a tough programme of fixtures. No doubt I should have explained the situation properly to the selectors, when they might have been dissuaded from taking what people told me was 'disciplinary action'.

I was still flabbergasted to hear on the telephone from a Pressman that I had been dropped from the squad. The selectors, I had believed, were my friends, yet none of them had thought to warn me of my impending omission.

To this day I have never been officially told the Big Five's side of the story.

England caught napping! Gareth Edwards puts Wales on course for victory with a try stolen from under the noses of the defenders.

Fearing that he would be the whipping-boy if anything went wrong, Bennett kept a low profile at Twickenham. His team-mates, however, declined to be put off by the strange vacillations of selectors. In running up their highest-ever winning margin at 'HQ' they owed much to another magnificent display from that twentieth-century Hammer of the English, J. P. R. Williams.

J. P. R. WILLIAMS: As memorable to me as my two tries in this game was an early tackle by Hignell which stopped him crossing for an opening score. He had support on each side, but tried to run through me. I didn't believe in allowing opponents to do that!

This tackle steadied the Welsh, and before long they were battering away at England's goal-line, where Gareth Edwards poached a try from beneath the noses of the opposing back row at a scrummage. Steve Fenwick converted, and Allan Martin soon kicked a long-range penalty goal.

Hignell briefly interrupted this sequence of scores with a penalty from 40 metres, but J. P. R. Williams would not be denied his customary Twickenham gesture.

J.P.R. scored a unique pair of tries in this game – but equally memorable to him was a tackle on Hignell which prevented a certain score by England.

J. P. R. WILLIAMS: My first try was created by 'J.J.', who did well to take a difficult pass from the midfield and jerk the ball back inside, all in one movement. I had five yards to cover and a number of defenders to beat, but my momentum was such that a full-length dive just got me to the corner flag.

A difficult conversion was prefectly executed by Fenwick, and although Hignell replied with another good penalty goal from 50 metres out the margin was nine points at the break.

Some observers thought that the Welsh pack tired a little during the second half, but none the less all England could achieve was a third Hignell penalty. The visitors reasserted their authority at the close, when J.P.R. raced up to accept a scissors pass from Bennett.

J. P. R. WILLIAMS: Phil was always very clever at this move. He made sure he had drawn the cover before giving the pass very quickly. So by the time I made my burst the England back row had committed itself to chasing him, and I found myself in plenty of space. I still needed to be at top speed, though, to beat Dave Duckham's cover tackle and score at the posts. The conversion was a formality for Steve Fenwick.

7 February 1976 at Cardiff

WALES   28 (2G 1T 1DG 3PG)
SCOTLAND   6 (1G)

Having been robbed effectively of a Grand Slam and
Triple Crown the previous season by defeat at
Murrayfield, this victory was the one the Welsh
players craved. It will be remembered not only for a
high score but also for indiscipline which referee
André Cuny was unable to quell. He also pulled a
muscle half an hour from no-side, limping along
thereafter at some remove from the action. His dis-
comfiture led to the reform whereby International

referees are now accompanied by two compatriot
touch judges, qualified to take control of a game if
required to do so.

Wales were quickly into the lead. Good possession gave Phil Bennett time to place his chip-kick
precisely for J. J. Williams to race in for a corner-
flag try which the stand-off converted. But the score
by no means unnerved the Scots, who were soon
moving the ball briskly towards the left from near
the half-way line. Now Andy Irvine's great pace
came into its own: speeding outside his wing, he just
evaded a despairing cover tackle by Mervyn Davies
to reach the line for a try which Douglas Morgan
converted with a grand kick.

J. P. R. WILLIAMS: It is a tragedy that Scotland never
turned Andy into a three-quarter. A brilliant runner, he
would have graced the centre or wing positions. But at

JPR: thundering upfield yet again!

full-back he lacked basic confidence under the high ball and in the tackle. These are basic defects in a key defender. Ask any forward!

His sense of adventure also created a tactical problem for Scotland's selectors. As long as Andy was their full-back they had to choose a defensively minded wing like Bruce Hay to cover his attacking exploits. This meant one less problem for the opposing defence.

A short while after the interval three penalties by Bennett and a dropped goal by Steve Fenwick had taken the home side well clear of the Scottish challenge, and given them the confidence to indulge in expansive play. Trevor Evans gave customary close support to a thrust by J. P. R. Williams, and was rewarded with a scoring pass at the end of some smart Welsh handling.

Then Gareth Edwards spread the cream on the cake with a smart try after J.P.R. had thundered upfield yet again and set up a maul.

GARETH EDWARDS: Truth to tell, it was near the end of the game and I was absolutely whacked! When I saw Phil Bennett close to the forwards I yelled, *'Cer mewn!'* — 'Get on in!' — and he played the role of scrum half to flick the ball out to me.

For one who was used to constant close attention from forwards you can understand that it was a luxury to find myself with some space around me. So I set off for the line, which was about 20 metres away. Douglas Morgan bought a big dummy, and by the time Scotland's wing Billy Steel realized that I was not going to pass to J. J. Williams it was too late — I'd reached the line.

The try was a record-equalling one, while Bennett's conversion to complete the scoring went one better.

MATCH 47

21 February 1976 in Dublin

IRELAND 9 (3PG)
WALES 34 (3G 1T 4PG)

FACT BOX

With 34 points, Wales broke the record they had set against Ireland only 12 months earlier. Gareth Edwards equalled Ken Jones's record 44 appearances for Wales and set a new scoring record with his 18th International try. Phil Bennett won his 20th cap, scored his first try for Wales and became the first to top 100 points for his country. His 19 points also brought him level with Jack Bancroft and Keith Jarrett for an individual total in one game. By winning his 37th cap Mervyn Davies overtook Denzil Williams's record for a Welsh forward.

Ireland A. H. Ensor, T. O. Grace (Captain), P. J. Lavery, C. M. H. Gibson, A. W. McMaster, B. J. McGann, D. M. Canniffe, P. A. Orr, J. Cantrell, P. O'Callaghan, M. I. Keane, R. F. Hakin, S. A. McKinney, W. P. Duggan, S. M. Deering.
Replacement: L. A. Moloney for Lavery.

Wales J. P. R. Williams (L. Welsh), T. G. R. Davies (Cardiff), R. W. R. Gravell (Llanelli), S. P. Fenwick (Bridgend), J. J. Williams (Llanelli), P. Bennett (Llanelli), G. O. Edwards (Cardiff), A. G. Faulkner (Pontypool), R. W. Windsor (Pontypool), G. Price (Pontypool), A. J. Martin (Aberavon), G. A. D. Wheel (Swansea), T. P. David (Pontypridd), T. M. Davies (Swansea, Captain), T. P. Evans (Swansea).

SCORERS
Ireland *Pens.* – McGann (3).
Wales *Tries* – Gerald Davies (2), Edwards, Bennett; *Cons.* – Bennett (3); *Pens.* – Bennett (3), Martin.

Referee: N. R. Sanson (SRU).

This must rank as one of the greatest victories by Wales in the 'seventies, standing comparison with the Grand Slam decider of 1971 in Paris. As a performance by a country playing away from home it may be bracketed with South Africa's 44–0 defeat of Scotland in 1951, the Paris win by Wales in 1975, and the big victories by New Zealand and Scotland at Cardiff in 1980 and 1982.

At the interval Ireland still seemed in with a chance. Barry McGann had placed three penalties, to which Allan Martin and Phil Bennett replied, and Wales owed a 10–9 lead to the opportunism of Gerald Davies.

GERALD DAVIES: I'm happy to recall my first try, if only because the Irish TV cameras missed most of it! A kick at goal by Allan Martin was wide, but an Irish defender delayed his clearance just too long and the ball rebounded from my chest over the line, where I touched it down. For once the routine and often fruitless chore of following up a penalty kick had paid off.

When attempting to charge down a kick, I used to aim my body at the point of impact between the kicker's boot and the ball. That way, I cut down the angles at which the ball could get past me, and made it unlikely that I would be penalized for a late tackle.

Mervyn Davies's half-time pep-talk encouraged the visitors to turn on a devastating display of positive rugby, which left their opponents breathless and well beaten.

MERVYN DAVIES: At half-time, remembering how I had been criticized in my early captaincy days for being too cautious, I told the boys, 'We've cracked them — let's enjoy ourselves now and play some rugby!'

I had a great team under me, and that's all they needed to hear.

A couple of penalties by Phil Bennett gave Wales confidence, and soon the floodgates were opened with another Gerald Davies try.

GERALD DAVIES: The Irish defenders were clinically taken out by the players inside me, and I was left with a simple overlap to exploit.

GARETH EDWARDS: At this stage, everybody seemed to be handling the ball, even tight forwards like Charlie Faulkner and Geoff Wheel. Ireland were all at sea, and when I put a chip kick into the 'box' behind a line-out, their defenders seemed too dazed to get under it. John Moloney finally got hold of the ball rather half-heartedly, but I ripped it from his grasp and crossed for our third try.

There was one more try to come, scored by Phil Bennett.

PHIL BENNETT: The credit for it must go to Ray Gravell, who put down Mike Gibson with a ferocious shoulder-charge. When I looped outside to receive his pass, I needed only a short sprint and a dummy to reach the line. Llanelli and Wales often profited from 'Grav's' physical presence in the midfield.

As I got up, Barry McGann said, 'Well done, Phil.' You don't often hear that kind of sporting sentiment on the field these days.

Gerald Davies in defence near the Welsh 22. Most of the action, though, was at Ireland's end of the field.

Three conversions by Bennett set the seal on a great performance by the Welsh. They had now secured a Triple Crown — could they go on to a Grand Slam?

GERALD DAVIES: The try-race between Gareth Edwards and me was hotting up now. The two I scored put me level with him and three predecessors, all of us having totalled 17 for our country. Then Gareth got another to give him the new record.

Later on, I could have caught him up again had Phil Bennett passed to me instead of dummying and crossing the line himself. I told Gareth that he must have paid Phil £10 for that!

MERVYN DAVIES: Late in the game, after Willie Duggan had been guilty of a short-arm tackle, I asked Phil Bennett to kick at goal. A bit surprised, since he had expected us to run the ball, he put the ball wide.

Afterwards I informed him that had he put the kick over, he would have set a new record for an individual points contribution in an International match, edging in front of Jack Bancroft and Keith Jarrett. His face fell a mile!

MATCH 48

6 March 1976 at Cardiff

WALES 19 (1T 5PG)
FRANCE 13 (1G 1T 1PG)

FACT BOX

By winning a 45th (consecutive) cap Gareth Edwards set a new Welsh record in a game when his country completed the Grand Slam for the seventh time, equalling England's record and creating a scoring record of 102 Championship points. Of this total Phil Bennett contributed 38 points, a new peak for Wales and a Championship record held jointly with Roger Hosen (England).

Some weeks after this match a brain haemorrhage brought about the premature retirement of Mervyn Davies. He won 38 caps and captained Wales to victory eight times in nine games.

Wales J. P. R. Williams (L. Welsh), T. G. R. Davies (Cardiff), R. W. R. Gravell (Llanelli), S. P. Fenwick (Bridgend), J. J. Williams (Llanelli), P. Bennett (Llanelli), G. O. Edwards (Cardiff), A. G. Faulkner (Pontypool), R. W. Windsor (Pontypool), G. Price (Pontypool), G. A. D. Wheel (Swansea), A. J. Martin (Aberavon), T. P. David (Pontypridd), T. M. Davies (Swansea, Captain), T. P. Evans (Swansea).
Replacement: F. M. D. Knill (Cardiff) for Price.

France M. Droitecourt, J-F. Gourdon, R. Bertranne, J. Pecune, J-L. Averous, J-P. Romeu, J. Fouroux (Captain), G. Cholley, A. Paco, R. Paparemborde, J-F. Imbernon, M. Palmie, J-P. Rives, J-P. Bastiat, J-C. Skrela.
Replacement: J-M. Aguirre for Droitecourt.

SCORERS
Wales *Try* – J. J. Williams;
Pens. – Bennett (2), Fenwick (2), Martin.
France *Tries* – Gourdon, Averous;
Con. – Romeu; *Pen.* – Romeu.

Referee: J. R. West (IRFU).

One of the hardest matches of the 'seventies ended with victory for Wales and the completion of a seventh Grand Slam. To great acclaim, Gareth

Edwards duly made his forty-fifth appearance for his country, moving above Ken Jones on the roll of honour, but the close marking of Skrela, Rives and his opposing scrum-half Fouroux prevented him from developing his usual free-flowing game.

GARETH EDWARDS: France's style this day was alien to their traditions. It amounted to ten-man rugby, with a big pack supported by kicking half-backs. As the game went on I also sensed that this French side were far less temperamental than those I had played against previously.

After four minutes an ambitious Welsh move from the 22-line broke down, and Romeu's quick intervention sent Gourdon speeding away on a 40-metre sprint to the line. Romeu converted.

GARETH EDWARDS: Handing France a lead on a plate could have been fatal, for the confidence they had gained came through in their play and they caused us many problems. But this Welsh XV was not one to panic. Basic ability and team-spirit had been cemented on our Japan tour the previous summer. We were a mature side, and were not going to be put out of our stride.

Phil Bennett kicked a penalty goal when the French offended at a line-out, and then came the best of the day's three tries. Graham Price peeled determinedly into midfield, and his team-mates arrived in force to win the maul. J. P. R. Williams was next into the fray, after which the ball reached Bennett.

PHIL BENNETT: At International level you do not expect to beat your man from a set-piece. But now I had the ball in my hand from broken play, the kind of situation where I liked to think that I was the master, and I knew I had to take on the defenders. They were off balance, and my couple of side-steps took me into space. The pass I sent to Steve Fenwick, however, had to be floated over the heads of the remaining couple of Frenchmen — and he did well to take it and put J. J. Williams in for an unconverted try.

Bennett and Allan Martin (from 50 metres) placed more penalties for Wales, but after his fine conversion Romeu's form fell away and he succeeded with only one out of four further attempts at goal before the interval.

In the second half France sent on Aguirre for Droitecourt, while Graham Price made way for Mike Knill of Cardiff RFC, who thus gained a first cap.

GARETH EDWARDS: Mike's presence on the replacements' bench was providential. At the time he was second only to Graham as a scrummager in Wales, so we knew when he came on that we would not be surrendering the initiative to France in the front row.

For a while Wales exerted unrelenting pressure which resulted in a series of near-misses, and one especially memorable move: Bennett, Gerald Davies, Fenwick, J. J. Williams and Tom David all handled in an attack which swept 70 metres upfield to end at France's goal-line. But a Fenwick penalty goal was all that rewarded these efforts, after which the French moved on to the attack.

GARETH EDWARDS: In earlier time French teams might have fallen apart under the kind of battering we had given this one. I have to salute the stubborn resistance that was put up.

France, however, added only one try, scored by Averous after tricky running from Pecune and a cleverly weighted chip-ahead by Aguirre. Fenwick's long penalty after the visitors' backs wandered off-side was an isolated gesture from a Welsh side with its back to the wall. The stalwart tackling of back-row men Tom David, Trevor Evans and Mervyn Davies was matched in the very last minute by an immense shoulder-charge upon Gourdon by J. P. R. Williams which catapulted the wing into touch on the Welsh goal-line. Victory had been hard-earned.

Gimlet-eyed, Phil Bennett sizes up the options ahead. The Llanelli star was always happiest running from broken play.

A few weeks after this game Mervyn Davies suffered the brain haemorrhage which forced his retirement from the game. He could, however, look back with pleasure and satisfaction on a well organized and directed Grand Slam campaign.

GARETH EDWARDS: 'Swerve' was resolute to the end. Early in his last game his calf muscle was trampled, and grew steadily more swollen and painful. Our physiotherapist Gerry Lewis wanted to take him off, but Mervyn preferred to stay with his men to the end.

He wasn't the most skilful footballer in the world. But he never made mistakes, and he never asked anyone to do something that he could not do himself — that is, he led by example.

He also understood that at this time we had a back division which ran itself. So he concentrated on maintaining a head of steam among his forwards, and was entirely successful.

Championship Table 1975–76

	P	W	D	L	PF	PA	Pts
WALES (1)	4	4	0	0	102	37	8
FRANCE (2)	4	3	0	1	82	37	6
SCOTLAND (2)	4	2	0	2	49	59	4
IRELAND (2)	4	1	0	3	31	87	2
ENGLAND (5)	4	0	0	4	42	86	0

Numbers in brackets indicate last season's positions.

8 January 1977 at Cardiff

WALES 25 (2G 1T 1DG 2PG)
IRELAND 9 (3PG)

FACT BOX

Gerald Davies equalled Gareth Edwards's record of 18 International tries.
Geoff Wheel and Willie Duggan became the first players to be sent off in a Five Nations' Championship match.

Wales J. P. R. Williams (Bridgend), T. G. R. Davies (Cardiff), S. P. Fenwick (Bridgend), D. H. Burcher (Newport), J. J. Williams (Lanelli), P. Bennett (Llanelli, Captain), G. O. Edwards (Cardiff), G. Shaw (Neath), R. W. Windsor (Pontypool), G. Price (Pontypool), A. J. Martin (Aberavon), G. A. D. Wheel (Swansea), T. P. Evans (Swansea), J. Squire (Newport), R. C. Burgess (Ebbw Vale).
Replacement: D. L. Quinnell (Llanelli) for Trevor Evans.

Ireland F. Wilson, T. O. Grace (Captain), A. R. McKibbin, J. A. McIlrath, D. St. J. Bowen, C. M. H. Gibson, R. J. McGrath, P. A. Orr, P. C. Whelan, T. A. Feighery, M. I. Keane, R. F. Hakin, S. A. McKinney, W. P. Duggan, S. M. Deering.
Replacement: B. O. Foley for Hakin.

SCORERS
Wales *Tries* – Gerald Davies, J. P. R. Williams, Burgess; *Cons.* – Bennett (2); *Pens.* – Bennett (2); *D.G.* – Fenwick.
Ireland *Pens.* – Gibson (3).
Sent off: Geoff Wheel (Wales) and Willie Duggan (Ireland) just before half-time.

Referee: N. R. Sanson (SRU).

Taking the view — for the time being — that prop Charlie Faulkner's best days were over, the selectors dropped him in favour of Glyn Shaw. New caps were awarded to Jeff Squire and David Burcher of Newport RFC and Ebbw Vale's Clive Burgess. The unavailability of Terry Cobner, who had led Wales in an unofficial Test match against Argentina the previous October, meant that for the first time Phil Bennett was to lead his country.

PHIL BENNETT: With his seniority, Gareth Edwards had probably expected to be restored as skipper. But despite the disappointment he must have felt, he lost no time in telephoning me with congratulations.

Although somewhat overwhelmed at the selectors' invitation, I was still thrilled.

The one-point victory over the Pumas had shown that there was much work to be done on the re-shaped Welsh side. Even now, three months later, the home team were still leaving their victory surge dangerously late. With twenty minutes of the match left, Ireland were in the lead by 9–6.

Ugly scenes had marred the early stages. There was sparring between the forwards, and then the punch-up as a result of which Geoff Wheel and Willie Duggan were sent off by referee Sanson.

PHIL BENNETT: One of my first duties as captain was to beg the referee not to send off the two players. 'I'm sorry, Phil,' he replied. 'I've already delivered a general warning, so I have no alternative.'

For an hour Ireland played with verve and considerable pace. Mistakes by Wales conceded two penalties to the 58-times-capped Mike Gibson and although Phil Bennett kicked two for Wales early in the second half, the slim Irishman completed a hat-trick after Allan Martin had barged at a line-out.

The flow of the game, already disturbed by the sendings-off, was further affected by the loss of Hakin and Trevor Evans, for whom Foley and Quinnell were replacements. Then at last Wales put some moves together. A clever change of direction by Steve Fenwick put Bennett into space. David Burcher stayed at his captain's elbow as he beat the Irish back row.

GERALD DAVIES: Dave was the link-man who gave me a scoring pass. Since he was off-balance at the time, I forgive him for sending it at daisy-top level!

Talking about passing, I liked the ball to come to me at chest-level, so that I could preserve the peripheral vision which is all-important for sighting defenders. My favourite centres were John Dawes and Mike Gibson, who not only delivered perfectly timed passes but also weighed up all the options which existed, both for them and for me.

Ray Gravell and Steve Fenwick were unfortunately labelled 'crash-ball' players as Internationals. But if you watched them at club level you realized that they too knew how to create space for team-mates.

For the first time Wales led, and, sensing that Ireland's will to resist was ebbing, J. P. R. Williams came up in attack.

One of the new Wales skipper Phil Bennett's first duties was to beg Norman Sanson not to send Geoff Wheel from the field. But the referee had no alternative.

J. P. R. WILLIAMS: A midfield miss-move created some space for me, but the pass I received was not easy to take. However, I managed to recover and get to the posts.

Playing for Wales this season was almost relaxing! I had returned from London to practise medicine in South Wales, and naturally rejoined Bridgend RFC. Here the fans seemed to expect me to work miracles in every game.

A cheeky dropped goal by Fenwick yielded three more points before Wales rounded off an onslaught which produced 19 points in twenty minutes. Bennett brought the ball to the right and linked with Gerald Davies, who cut inside and gave a pass to Clive Burgess. The flanker put his head back and beat two defenders in a 20-metre gallop to the posts for a debut try. Bennett kicked the conversion.

MATCH 50

5 February 1977 at Parc des Princes

FRANCE 16 (1G 1T 2PG)
WALES 9 (3PG)

FACT BOX

This was the 50th meeting between Wales and France.

France J-M. Aguirre, D. Harize, R. Bertranne, F. Sangali, J-L. Averous, J-P. Romeu, J. Fouroux (Captain), G. Cholley, A. Paco, R. Paparemborde, J-F. Imbernon, M. Palmie, J-P. Rives, J-P. Bastiat, J-C. Skrela.

Wales J. P. R. Williams (Bridgend), T. G. R. Davies (Cardiff), S. P. Fenwick (Bridgend), D. H. Burcher (Newport), J. J. Williams (Llanelli), P. Bennett (Llanelli, Captain), G. O. Edwards (Cardiff), G. Shaw (Neath), R. W. Windsor (Pontypool), G. Price (Pontypool), A. J. Martin (Aberavon), D. L. Quinnell (Llanelli), R. C. Burgess (Ebbw Vale), J. Squire (Newport), T. J. Cobner (Pontypool).
Replacement: G. L. Evans (Newport) for Gerald Davies.

SCORERS
France *Tries* – Harize, Skrela; *Con.* – Romeu; *Pens.* – Romeu (2).
Wales *Pens.* – Fenwick (3).

Referee: A. M. Hosie (SRU).

Pounded for eighty minutes by one of the biggest packs ever to play for France, the Champions met their match in this all-action Paris spectacular. The home forwards took the scrummages comfortably, while the lines-out were dominated by Palmie, Imbernon and Bastiat.

GARETH EDWARDS: Bastiat in particular now emerged as a tremendous force. Without Mervyn Davies to give him a run for his money he was head and shoulders above the other players at lines-out. And given regular, high-quality possession, Jacques Fouroux and Jean-Pierre Romeu gained 50 or 60 metres with their kicking. It was soul-destroying!

The unavailability of Geoff Wheel (suspended after his Cardiff sending-off) and Trevor Evans (injured) brought Derek Quinnell and Terry Cobner back into the fray. Gareth Evans of Newport RFC, who replaced the concussed Gerald Davies soon after the interval, was a new cap for Wales.

Gareth Edwards spent his first half-hour putting in non-stop relieving kicks in the face of France's opening offensive, so that it was much against the run of play when Steve Fenwick gave the visitors a three-point lead with a penalty goal after thirty-three minutes. The culprit, falling offside at a line-out, had been French stand-off half Romeu, who made amends with a short penalty to tie the score at the interval.

Fenwick raised the hopes of Welsh supporters with a second penalty, but now the French bent themselves to the business of scoring tries. First came a colossal drive by number 8 Bastiat which forced Wales to concede a goal-line scrummage.

GARETH EDWARDS: Jean-Claude Skrela now picked up and drove through his pack for a try — but I had big reservations about it. First, was it legal? — that is, did the forwards in front of Skrela become accidentally offside?

Secondly, did the flanker ground the ball? Scots referee Alan Hosie ruled that he did — but in my opinion Mr Hosie was unsighted, and should have given the defending side the benefit of the doubt.

Before long an ambitious Welsh counter-attack broke down, and again Bastiat went surging through the visitors' ranks towards the Welsh corner flag, where he was bravely tackled by Phil Bennett. From this position, however, France spun the ball faultlessly along their three-quarter line, and wing Harize was given just enough space to reach the flag. Romeu's conversion attempt was wide, and soon a short-arm tackle by Bastiat allowed Fenwick to close the gap to three points with his third penalty.

J. P. R. WILLIAMS: Despite this, I had a perpetual sinking feeling during this game that the French were in the driving seat.

GARETH EDWARDS: On the contrary, I was surprised that the French had not been able to get completely clear. We were never really out of it until the final whistle, and I believed that we were going to sneak a win that we didn't deserve at all. Perhaps we would have done so had Phil Bennett been closer to his usual form and put over a couple of penalties which he ought to have kicked.

Destined to complete a Grand Slam this winter, however, France made certain of the spoils through a late penalty goal by Romeu.

Allan Martin wins a line-out duel.

MATCH 51

5 March 1977 at Cardiff

WALES 14 (2T 2PG)
ENGLAND 9 (3PG)

A first cap for Clive Williams *(centre, with ball)*. **Gareth Edwards says he was the cornerstone of a pack that gave England a hiding.**

FACT BOX

Gareth Edwards again nosed ahead of Gerald Davies in the try-race, scoring number 19 for Wales.

Gerald, along with J. P. R. Williams, made a 40th International appearance.

Wales J. P. R. Williams (Bridgend), T. G. R. Davies (Cardiff), S. P. Fenwick (Bridgend), D. H. Burcher (Newport), J. J. Williams (Llanelli), P. Bennett (Llanelli, Captain), G. O. Edwards (Cardiff), C. Williams (Aberavon), R. W. Windsor (Pontypool), G. Price (Pontypool), A. J. Martin (Aberavon), G. A. D. Wheel (Swansea), R. C. Burgess (Ebbw Vale), D. L. Quinnell (Llanelli), T. J. Cobner (Pontypool).

England A. J. Hignell, P. J. Squires, B. J. Corless, C. P. Kent, M. A. C. Slemen, M. J. Cooper, M. Young, R. J. Cowling, P. J. Wheeler, F. E. Cotton, W. B. Beaumont, N. E. Horton, P. J. Dixon, R. M. Uttley (Captain), M. Rafter.

SCORERS
Wales *Tries* – Edwards, J. P. R. Williams; *Pens.* – Fenwick (2).
England *Pens.* – Hignell (3).

Referee: D. I. H. Burnett (IRFU).

Wales made adjustments to their team for England's visit to the National Ground. Geoff Wheel returned at lock, with Derek Quinnell ousting Jeff Squire from the number 8 position. Glyn Shaw was dropped in favour of Charlie Faulkner, only for the Pontypool prop to be ruled out by injury. Clive Williams of Aberavon RFC won a first cap in his place.

GARETH EDWARDS: Clive, a quiet man, was an absolute revelation! Having seen his debut from close range, I can say that he was the cornerstone of a pack that not only held the Englishmen but gave them a hiding into the bargain.

Before the match even fervent Welsh supporters had been saying that it was Wales's turn to be 'done over'. The damage, people said, would start up front, where Roger Uttley, Fran Cotton, Bill Beaumont and Nigel Horton would eat their opponents alive!

The visitors did acquit themselves well for much of the game, only to succumb in the final quarter — when their cause was not helped by a back injury which hampered their number 8 forward and captain, Uttley. Alistair Hignell gave them a good

118

start with a pair of penalty goals, but soon Gareth Edwards seized a chance to show what irresistible form he was in.

GARETH EDWARDS: Our forwards heeled the ball and then held it at a scrummage five metres from England's line. The opposing back row had to stay down and shove in case Wales went for a pushover try, so when I finally whisked the ball from behind Derek Quinnell's heels and drove for the line there was only a wing to beat. It was a one-to-one confrontation of the kind I relished — and I got the try!

Penalties by Fenwick, Hignell, and Fenwick again saw the fourth quarter arrive with the home team's lead a mere point at 10–9 and the game seemingly capable of being won by either side. Now, however, Welsh stamina was to prove the decisive factor,

Allan Martin and Geoff Wheel providing gilt-edged possession which permitted their half-backs to maintain a tactical stranglehold.

The decisive moment came fifteen minutes from time. David Burcher broke cleanly through a gap in midfield, and found ready support from J. P. R. Williams, who took advantage of clever running off the ball by right-wing Gerald Davies to side-step the corner-flagging defenders and cross the line for a fifth International try against England. The conversion attempt failed, but 14 points were just enough to give Wales a hard-fought victory.

BARRY JOHN: The victory seemed to have been a laborious affair. And instead of going for a knock-out, Wales remained vulnerable until the final whistle to a breakaway converted try by England.

MATCH 52

19 March 1977 at Murrayfield

SCOTLAND 9 (1G 1DG)
WALES 18 (2G 2PG)

FACT BOX

Wales took the Triple Crown for the 14th time, equalling England's record.
Gareth Edwards won his 49th consecutive cap, beating a world record held by Ireland's Willie John McBride.

Scotland A. R. Irvine, W. B. B. Gammell, J. M. Renwick, A. G. Cranston, D. Shedden, I. R. McGeechan (Captain), D. W. Morgan, J. McLauchlan, D. F. Madsen, A. B. Carmichael, I. A. Barnes, A. F. McHarg, W. S. Watson, D. S. M. MacDonald, M. A. Biggar.

Wales J. P. R. Williams (Bridgend), T. G. R. Davies (Cardiff), S. P. Fenwick (Bridgend), D. H. Burcher (Newport), J. J. Williams (Llanelli), P. Bennett (Llanelli, Captain), G. O. Edwards (Cardiff), C. Williams (Aberavon), R. W. Windsor (Pontypool), G. Price (Pontypool), A. J. Martin (Aberavon), G. A. D. Wheel (Swansea), T. J. Cobner (Pontypool), D. L. Quinnell (Llanelli), R. C. Burgess (Ebbw Vale).

SCORERS
Scotland *Try* — Irvine; *Con.* — Irvine; *D.G.* — McGeechan.
Wales *Tries* — J. J. Williams, Bennett; *Cons.* — Bennett (2); *Pens.* — Bennett (2).

Referee: G. Domercq (FRF).

GARETH EDWARDS: Waving in front of our selectors the promoters' guarantee of my return for the Murrayfield Triple Crown match, I had flown off to Atlanta, Georgia, for a Superstars TV tournament. But as I lined up for the hundred metres' sprint it suddenly dawned on me how much the game due to take place 5,000 miles away meant to me, and how terrible I would feel if I pulled a hamstring and had to withdraw from the Welsh team.

I took that hundred metres at a canter, and told the TV people that, with many regrets, I wanted to return home immediately. The Murrayfield game was one that I would have hated to miss!

This match was generally agreed to be the best Championship encounter of the winter, containing much positive, imaginative rugby which led to tries of superlative quality. Scarcely had many fans glanced up from their programmes than Ian McGeechan was putting Scotland into the lead with a deft dropped goal.

By half-time a Phil Bennett penalty goal had tied the score, but Wales fell behind again soon afterwards to a great try initiated by Douglas Morgan. Breaking flat from a scrummage, the scrum-half sent Jim Renwick speeding through a gap in the Welsh midfield. Andy Irvine took a pass, cut back past a knot of defenders, and went over at the posts for a try which he himself converted. It was somewhat against the run of play when Gareth Edwards and Phil Bennett set up a try on the blind side for J. J. Williams, but there was no doubting the quality of Bennett's conversion from near to touch. Soon he put Wales into the lead with a further penalty goal; and then came one of the great moments of 1977.

One of the great moments of 1977: Phil Bennett rounds off a superlative handling movement to score the decisive try for Wales. His team-mates are J. J. Williams (11) and David Burcher.

PHIL BENNETT: The Scots were angry at falling behind for the first time, and they started throwing everything into attack. The try we produced to clinch the match was out of this world — but just before it, the Welsh defence was rubber-legged with exhaustion.

GERALD DAVIES: The Scots had switched the ball across our ten-metre line four or five times, putting us on the rack. Finally J.P.R. fell on a loose ball inside the 22-area and scooped it to Steve Fenwick.

PHIL BENNETT: At that moment I'd have settled for a big, relieving touch-kick. But Gerald bobbed up at Steve's elbow — and as he took the pass he must have sensed that the opposition were as tired as ourselves, and would be slow covering back.

GERALD DAVIES: Everybody had been helping in defence wherever they were needed — that's why I was in midfield and able to accept a pass from Steve. My main consideration was to maximize our use of this scrap of loose possession, for the Scots had been winning everything for the previous few minutes. So I set off, gaining momentum as I handed off Dougie Morgan's dog-tired attempt to tackle me, and passed to Phil Bennett. Thereafter I stood back to admire the slick inter-passing with centres Dave Burcher and, again, Steve Fenwick which put Phil into space.

PHIL BENNETT: By the time I got the ball from Steve there were only Bill Gammell and 'Mighty Mouse' McLauchlan to beat, and it was not difficult to catch them off balance and race on for a try at the posts. After putting the ball down I lay prone for an extra couple of seconds; I was relishing the fact that we had moved two vital scores ahead — but I was also trying desperately to summon the energy to get to my feet!

Bennett himself chipped over the conversion; and that evening learned that he would captain the British Isles on tour that summer. Would New Zealand take its toll of Welsh resilience during the summer of 1977? Or could this brand of Murrayfield magic be reproduced in the New Year?

Championship Table 1976–77

	P	W	D	L	PF	PA	Pts
FRANCE (2)	4	4	0	0	58	21	8
WALES (1)	4	3	0	1	66	43	6
ENGLAND (5)	4	2	0	2	42	24	4
SCOTLAND (3)	4	1	0	3	39	85	2
IRELAND (4)	4	0	0	4	33	65	0

Numbers in brackets indicate last season's positions.

4 February 1978 at Twickenham

ENGLAND 6 (2PG)
WALES 9 (3PG)

FACT BOX

Inevitably! — Gareth Edwards's 50th consecutive cap.
And Phil Bennett took his points total for Wales to 150.

England   A. J. Hignell. P. J. Squires,
B. J. Corless, P. W. Dodge, M. A. C. Slemen,
J. P. Horton, M. Young, B. G. Nelmes,
P. J. Wheeler, M. A. Burton, W. B. Beaumont
(Captain), N. E. Horton, R. J. Mordell,
J. P. Scott, M. Rafter.

Wales   J. P. R. Williams (Bridgend),
T. G. R. Davies (Cardiff), R. W. R. Gravell
(Llanelli), S. P. Fenwick (Bridgend),
J. J. Williams (Llanelli), P. Bennett (Llanelli,
Captain), G. O. Edwards (Cardiff),
A. G. Faulkner (Pontypool), R. W. Windsor
(Pontypool), G. Price (Pontypool), A. J. Martin
(Aberavon), G. A. D. Wheel (Swansea),
J. Squire (Newport), D. L. Quinnell (Llanelli),
T. J. Cobner (Pontypool).

SCORERS
England   *Pens.* — Hignell (2).
Wales   *Pens.* — Bennett (3).

Referee: N. R. Sanson (SRU).

The technique of Allan Martin — dependable for Wales at the lines-out for nearly a decade.

Twickenham's car-parks were awash with rainwater as a capacity crowd arrived for this match. Despite being decided by penalty goals, the day's muddy contest would contain much to interest the connoisseur — not to mention a fiftieth appearance for his country by Gareth Edwards.

GARETH EDWARDS: Naturally, this was a game in which I wanted desperately to be on the winning side. But as drizzle started falling on London soon after breakfast, I knew that the manner of winning was not likely to be spectacular. In damp, greasy conditions control would be all-important.

The visitors undoubtedly had the players to gain such control. Apart from Llanelli's Raymond Gravell (already the holder of nine caps), who returned to displace David Burcher, all of them had been in the Championship runners-up XV the previous year. Phil Bennett retained the captaincy.

The English began aggressively, monopolizing what clean possession could be secured with the slippery ball. After eight minutes the Pontypool front row, restored intact to the National XV, conceded a penalty which Hignell goaled, but within a minute an error at the base of England's scrummage allowed Bennett to equalize. Seeking his 'Twickenham try', J. P. R. Williams was halted three metres from England's goal-line after a determined sortie, and Slemen ran dangerously for the home side, but the next three points again came from the boot: Wales barged at a line-out, and Hignell gave his side a 6–3 interval lead.

Soon Bennett put over another penalty goal, which stung England to a series of furious attacks. Half-backs Horton and Young steered play to the Welsh line, where Beaumont and his men laid a protracted siege. When Wales at last lifted the pressure it was to find that England had shot their bolt.

Not until five minutes from no-side, however, did they finally give best. The strain of a continuous bombardment of up-and-unders — mainly from Gareth Edwards, but also from Bennett, Gerald

Besides kicking three vital penalty goals Phil Bennett showed up well in defence. Here (on ground at right) **he has got across to halt a dangerous thrust by Mike Slemen.**

Davies and J. P. R. Williams — caused their concentration to snap. At a ruck 25 metres from their posts they conceded the penalty with which Bennett won the match.

The critics agreed that Gareth Edwards could claim much credit for his side's narrow victory. Exploiting the second-half breeze, he nursed his forwards upfield with astute — and often immense — tactical kicks, drawing England's defenders mercilessly from corner to corner and sapping their will to counter-attack. It was surely one of the scrum-half's most masterly displays, keeping Wales within range of the opposition's posts, and thus making it possible ultimately for Bennett to place his winning goal.

MERVYN DAVIES: The Welsh effort on this day was not as well organized as I would have liked. It struck me that players were striving for themselves, not for the team.

To give an example: in my time, when forwards gripped an opponent who held the ball, two of them would seize an arm each and make it possible for a third team-mate to gain possession. On this day at Twickenham it struck me that all eight of the pack wanted to have the glory of handling the ball. Craft and method seemed to have given way to selfishness.

MATCH 54

18 February 1978 at Cardiff

WALES 22 (4T 1DG 1PG)
SCOTLAND 14 (2T 2PG)

GARETH EDWARDS: Even those taking part in the fast, vigorous game found it hard to warm up properly, for the icy wind seemed to cut right through us. I had seldom known conditions so difficult and unpleasant.

Nevertheless, Edwards replied to Douglas Morgan's opening penalty goal with an unconverted try — his twentieth for his country — to give Wales the lead, before Scotland nosed ahead again. Cranston had hitherto spent his time beating off the midfield crash-ball assaults of Steve Fenwick and Ray Gravell, but now his quick use of good Scottish possession made room for Bruce Hay to join the move, and Jim Renwick was sent speeding in for a try which Morgan could not convert.

Just before the interval Wales began the twenty-

A familiar sight – empty, clutching fingers and frustrated expressions as Gareth Edwards stretches out for his twentieth International try.

Many observers thought this the coldest day on which they had watched rugby football. During the match the temperature dropped rapidly, and some half-hour after no-side the snow which had threatened all day began falling. Many Scottish supporters were trapped by a blizzard which forced them to spend an extra two or three days in Wales. The hospitality accorded by their hosts, however, soon restored morale which had sunk during a match resulting in yet another home win for the men in red.

minute blitz which won them the match. After Edwards had run a free kick inside Scotland's 22-area, Ray Gravell scythed through for his first International try. Then Douglas Morgan carelessly fly-hacked a loose ball towards the opposing half-backs, and Edwards's swift pass found Bennett perfectly placed for a dropped goal.

Steve Fenwick was next to score, Bennett added a penalty goal, and then Derek Quinnell delighted the crowd with a dramatic 20-metre dash for a try.

MERVYN DAVIES: It was his first for Wales, and was spectacular enough to make me wish I had scored one like it in an International game! However, I have to say that it owed much to pathetic Scottish tackling. Had Alastair McHarg just given Derek a push, he was bound to have stepped into touch.

The try remained unconverted, but with twenty-five minutes of the match still left the home team seemed to lose the will to increase their lead.

BARRY JOHN: The victory should have been a fifty-pointer, but Wales stopped stretching their opponents. I put some of the blame on Gareth for deciding tactics in advance and not playing each ball on merit. Perhaps, for once in his career, he was thinking of solo tries and record-breaking feats!

GARETH EDWARDS: Barry had a nice warm seat in the stand . . . ! But there's some truth in what he says. I tried to break on my own too often, looking for tries that weren't there.

So it was Scotland who won applause for a series of enterprising counter-attacks from within their own half that helped to give their score respectability. Douglas Morgan kicked a second penalty, and Alan Tomes forced his way over for a good try after gaining possession at a line-out. By the close, however, the home side had dug into its reserves of stamina, and was again camped menacingly in Scotland's 22-area.

GERALD DAVIES: Wings deserve pity on cold days like this one. After the game some of us spent half an hour restoring circulation to our numbed limbs!

4 March 1978 in Dublin
IRELAND 16 (1T 1DG 3PG)
WALES 20 (2T 4PG)

J. J. Williams eludes Tony Ensor's attempted tackle to cross at the corner — and for Wales the worst is over!

FACT BOX

Lansdowne Road celebrated 100 years of International rugby this season – but Wales also sipped champagne after clinching a unique third Triple Crown in successive seasons. What is more, the same 15 players went through the three matches of 1978 unchanged.
Although Gerald Davies equalled Ken Jones's Welsh record for a Welsh three-quarter of 44 caps, the individual thunder was stolen by Ireland's evergreen Mike Gibson who won a world record 64th cap.

Ireland A. H. Ensor, C. M. H. Gibson, A. R. McKibbin, P. P. McNaughton, A. C. McLennan, A. J. P. Ward, J. J. Moloney (Captain), P. A. Orr, P. C. Whelan, E. M. J. Byrne, M. I. Keane, H. W. Steele, S. A. McKinney, W. P. Duggan, J. F. Slattery.

Wales J. P. R. Williams (Bridgend), T. G. R. Davies (Cardiff), R. W. R. Gravell (Llanelli), S. P. Fenwick (Bridgend), J. J. Williams (Llanelli), P. Bennett (Llanelli, Captain), G. O. Edwards (Cardiff), A. G. Faulkner (Pontypool), R. W. Windsor (Pontypool), G. Price (Pontypool), A. J. Martin (Aberavon), G. A. D. Wheel (Swansea), J. Squire (Newport), D. L. Quinnell (Llanelli), T. J. Cobner (Pontypool).

SCORERS
Ireland *Try* – Moloney; *Pens.* – Ward (3); *D.G.* – Ward.
Wales *Tries* – Fenwick, J. J. Williams; *Pens.* – Fenwick (4).

Referee: G. Domercq (FRF).

An unchanged Welsh XV set off for Dublin in pursuit of an unprecedented third Triple Crown in succession. But newcomer Tony Ward and veteran Mike Gibson were stars in an Irish side which had

beaten Scotland and succumbed by a single point in Paris. The visitors knew that the encounter would be hard.

PHIL BENNETT: It was more than that, it was warfare. It left such a bad taste in my mouth that I prefer not to discuss it.

After 40 minutes it seemed that Ireland's traditional fire had been extinguished. True, Ward had kicked two penalties, but Steve Fenwick had three to his credit. He had also scored a grand unconverted try, stretching his legs to outpace the defence after Wales won a loose ball beneath Ireland's posts.

GARETH EDWARDS: We led 13–6 at half-time. But the Irish had given us four gifts, including allowing Steve to make an outside break for a try! I said to Gerald Davies, 'There's something fishy about this game. It doesn't feel right.' My fears were well founded.

Now Moss Keane and Fergus Slattery revitalized their colleagues by example. Moloney and Ward at half-back profited from better-quality possession, and the latter soon found time and space in which to

drop a goal. He followed this with a towering punt which came down awkwardly for J. P. R. Williams on the Welsh goal-line. The full-back took the ball calmly, only to slice his clearance across the in-goal area, where Moloney won a hectic race for the touchdown. The conversion attempt failed, but after a gallant recovery Ireland were now on level terms.

GARETH EDWARDS: It was the manner in which they had got there that upset us. 'Slats', as we called him affectionately, seemed to go berserk, and stopped at nothing to subdue us. His mania infected the other Irish forwards, who let fly with everything they possessed — boots, knuckles, fingernails, elbows.

It was painful and exhausting. Further, we got no protection from referee Georges Domercq of France. His main idea was to keep the game flowing and maintain his reputation for encouraging fluent play.

We reeled under this battering, like a champion boxer caught on the ropes, until ten minutes from time. It was then that I sensed that the Irish were spent: Bobby Windsor and the other forwards mopped up a loose ball that Ireland should have retained — and I thought, 'We're back in with a chance! The worst is over.'

Soon indeed, Edwards frustrated the Irish defenders with an overhead pass which gave Fenwick enough time and space to flick the ball on to J. J. Williams, who sped in for an unconverted try. Fenwick put over another penalty goal (reaching 16 points for the day), to which Ward replied, after which Wales held on doggedly to their narrow lead.

GARETH EDWARDS: The forward battle was so gruelling that twenty minutes after the final whistle our pack still hadn't digested the fact that we had achieved the impossible — a third Triple Crown on the trot!

Gerald Davies and I stripped, went for our shower, rubbed ourselves dry and came back into the changing-room to find Terry Cobner and the rest still slumped on the bench, muddy boots and all. They were totally drained of energy.

Undoubtedly this was the most exhausting game I ever played in, and pushed me towards a retirement decision. As I looked around at my team-mates I thought, 'There's no way I could endure this sort of afternoon again.'

A late tackle by J. P. R. Williams on Mike Gibson during the first half prompted the crowd to boo him each time he subsequently took part in the play. Did this action sour the game's spirit irreversibly?

J. P. R. WILLIAMS: Although my tackle was late, it was not deliberate — rather a reflex action. I think the Irish players understood this, and certainly Mike accepted my apology immediately after the game, like the fine sportsman that he is.

The most regrettable thing is that the incident was between J.P.R. and Gibbo. Had it involved two lesser known players I doubt if it would have attracted anything like the attention it did.

MATCH 56

18 March 1978 at Cardiff

WALES 16 (1G 1T 2DG)
FRANCE 7 (1T 1DG)

FACT BOX

This was the last International match for half-back partners Gareth Edwards and Phil Bennett, the former retiring subsequently from all rugby football, the latter from representative matches. The pair played together 24 times (25 counting the Murrayfield match of 1975 when Bennett came on as replacement for John Bevan) and broke the record for Welsh half backs set by Edwards and his previous partner Barry John. Edwards retired after captaining Wales 13 times, Bennett after eight times.
Bennett's ten points broke Tom Kiernan's European record of 158 points in Internationals and set a new mark of 166 — which, when added to his British Isles total of 44 Test points, also surpassed Don Clarke's world best of 207 for New Zealand.
Wales won the Grand Slam under Bennett for a record eighth time, finishing as Five Nations' champions for the twentieth time.

Wales J. P. R. Williams (Bridgend), J. J. Williams (Llanelli), R. W. R. Gravell (Llanelli), S. P. Fenwick (Bridgend), G. L. Evans (Newport), P. Bennett (Llanelli, Captain), G. O. Edwards (Cardiff), A. G. Faulkner (Pontypool), R. W. Windsor (Pontypool), G. Price (Pontypool), A. J. Martin (Aberavon), G. A. D. Wheel (Swansea), J. Squire (Newport), D. L. Quinnell (Llanelli), T. J. Cobner (Pontypool).

France J-M. Aguirre, D. Bustaffa, R. Bertranne, C. Belascain, G. Noves, B. Vivies, J. Gallion, G. Cholley, A. Paco, R. Paparemborde, F. Haget, M. Palmie, J-P. Rives, J-P. Bastiat (Captain), J-C. Skrela.

SCORERS
Wales Tries – Bennett (2); *Con.* – Bennett; *D. Gs.* – Edwards, Fenwick.
France *Try* – Skrela; *D. G.* – Vivies.

Referee: A. Welsby (RFU).

Wales had to pull out all the stops to earn the toughest Grand Slam of the decade. A fortnight after the exhausting fixture against Ireland the players — many of whom took part in gruelling WRU cup-ties on the intervening Saturday — did wonderfully well to overcome a French side which had won its first three games and was also bidding for a Grand Slam.

GARETH EDWARDS: People often ask me whether I knew as I came out of the tunnel that this fifty-third match as Wales's scrum-half would be my last. The answer is that I had not at this point made up my mind to retire. But things had reached the point where, I admit, I was just a bit fearful of having a bad game and being remembered as the man who played once too often for Wales.

In the event, both Gareth Edwards and Phil Bennett made final appearances for their country.

Not for the first time in the series of fixtures, it was France who began in a higher gear. Spurred on by an ear-bursting crescendo of trumpetings from the terraces, they set up a maul near the Welsh line, through which Skrela broke for an unconverted try. When Vivies added a dropped goal it was clear that Wales would have to play particularly well to preserve an unbeaten record against European opposition in Cardiff which stretched back to 1968.

PHIL BENNETT: This was a vital time for me to contribute my first try. A strike against the head by Bobby Windsor allowed Allan Martin to scoop the ball to me. Although a Frenchman stuck out an arm as I went for the line, I had enough speed to brush it away.
Psychologically my conversion was just as important, giving us the certainty that our next score of any kind would wipe out France's lead.

Edwards, meanwhile, was fighting his duel with Jérôme Gallion, hailed by the Tricolors as their new world-beating scrum half. The Welshman moved ahead on points by striking a superb dropped goal from 30 metres, clean line-out possession having given him space to steer the ball just inside the right-hand post.

GARETH EDWARDS: Gallion paid me a nice compliment afterwards. He said, 'It was nice to play against you. Today, you were the teacher.' I appreciated that.

Next Bennett increased the Welsh lead by rounding off what was arguably the best move produced by Wales through the winter. Ray Gravell probed dangerously in the midfield, after which Steve Fenwick switched Edwards away on a long run towards the opposite corner flag. His awkward pass to J. J. Williams was expertly gathered, and equally cleverly whisked inside for Bennett to gather and score.

One of Phil Bennett's two tries in his last game for Wales: 'A good way of saying thank you.'

PHIL BENNETT: Although I did not finalize the decision to leave International rugby until later in the year, looking back I am glad to have contributed two tries in my last game for Wales. That seemed a good way of saying thankyou for 29 caps and a whole lot of fun.

In the second half France produced some splendid combined play in which first Aguirre and then Bastiat were guilty of knocking on with the Welsh defence at sixes and sevens. But it was not the visitors' day. Wales weathered the storm, and went back on to the offensive for a final quarter of an hour. Steve Fenwick's dropped goal was icing on a tasty Grand Slam cake.

GARETH EDWARDS: As we left the field Jean-Pierre Rives gripped my hand and said affectionately, 'Gareth — you old fox! Wait till Paris next year!'

I said, 'Yes, of course.' But in my heart of hearts I knew that there would be no next year, in Paris or anywhere else. I had played rugby out of my system.

All the signs pointed towards a prudent retirement decision. We had won a 'Triple Triple Crown'. I had participated in a third Grand Slam. My total of caps had passed the half-century mark. And perhaps the most important factor of all — I had stayed free of serious injury, and never missed a match. I told the selectors that I would not be available for the forthcoming tour of Australia.

Championship Table 1977–78

	P	W	D	L	PF	PA	Pts
WALES (2)	4	4	0	0	67	43	8
FRANCE (1)	4	3	0	1	51	47	6
ENGLAND (3)	4	2	0	2	42	33	4
IRELAND (5)	4	1	0	3	46	54	2
SCOTLAND (4)	4	0	0	4	39	68	0

Numbers in brackets indicate last season's positions.

11 June 1978 at Brisbane

AUSTRALIA 18 (1G 4PG)
WALES 8 (2T)

FACT BOX

In his 45th International match Gerald Davies became the most-capped Welsh three-quarter, and scored his 19th International try.

Australia L. E. Monaghan, P. G. Batch, A. G. Slack, M. Knight, P. J. Crowe, P. E. McLean, R. G. Hauser, S. C. Finnane, P. A. Horton, S. J. Pilecki, D. J. Hillhouse, G. Fay, G. Cornelson, M. E. Loane, A. A. Shaw (Captain).

Wales J. P. R. Williams (Bridgend), T. G. R. Davies (Cardiff), S. P. Fenwick (Bridgend), R. W. R. Gravell (Llanelli), J. J. Williams (Llanelli), W. G. Davies (Cardiff), D. B. Williams (Newport), A. G. Faulkner (Pontypool), R. W. Windsor (Pontypool), G. Price (Pontypool), G. A. D. Wheel (Swansea), A. J. Martin (Aberavon), T. J. Cobner (Pontypool, Captain), D. L. Quinnell (Llanelli), J. Squire (Newport). *Replacement:* S. M. Lane (Cardiff) for Jeff Squire.

SCORERS
Australia *Try* – Crowe; *Con.* – McLean; *Pens.* – McLean (4).
Wales *Tries* – Gerald Davies, Brynmor Williams.

Referee: R. T. Burnett (Queensland).

The excuses were legion: Wales had just lost the services of world-class half-backs Gareth Edwards and Phil Bennett; the team were exhausted after an extraordinarily hard Grand Slam campaign; they were over-confident; the quality of the Australian opposition had been gravely underestimated.

J. P. R. WILLIAMS: One Welsh excuse is really valid — our anger at the choice of Bob Burnett to referee the Test. He had just made an awful mess of controlling our game with Queensland which, incidentally, we won.

GERALD DAVIES: I agree. The provincial game had given cause to doubt both the competence and the impartiality of Mr Burnett.

J. P. R. WILLIAMS: On tours in which I had previously taken part it was the practice to offer the visitors a four-man panel of officials to choose from. When the Australian authorities said Wales must accept Mr Burnett, our players mutinied and voted to return home. Had Clive Rowlands, the manager, acted as we wished and taken our party to the airport I believe the Aussies would have climbed down and appointed someone else to do the game. But Clive gave in first.

GERALD DAVIES: Never had I known such acrimony in the build-up to an important rugby match. It was no wonder that we could not give a good account of ourselves. From the start we were mystified and angered by Mr Burnett's rulings.

Observers noted that five of the first six penalty awards in the Test went Australia's way. Paul McLean kicked goals from 20 and 30 metres to pressurize the visitors and discourage them from developing adventurous, constructive rugby. Once

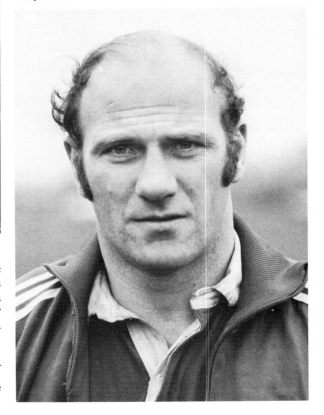

Terry Cobner: the first and only time he captained Wales.

A furious run by Ray Gravell paves the way for a Welsh try.

they did so, however, a score resulted. Bobby Windsor bobbed up as link-man between Steve Fenwick and Gareth Davies, Phil Bennett's successor at stand-off half.

GERALD DAVIES: Gareth's diagonal kick was perfectly placed. My marker, Phil Crowe, must have felt sure it would roll into touch. Instead it popped back infield for me to gather and score an unconverted try.

Soon, however, a ruck offence by Wales allowed McLean to complete a hat-trick of penalties, and give his side a 9–4 interval lead. The gap narrowed again fifteen minutes into the second half, when Fenwick was once more responsible for a clever switch of direction. Co-centre Ray Gravell carried on the attack furiously, and found Brynmor Williams with an inside pass. On his International debut, the scrum-half crossed for a try which again remained unconverted.

Australia pulled away from the European champions, however, when J. P. R. Williams was caught in possession. The Wallaby forwards reached the position briskly and moved the ball to wing Phil Crowe, who had enough room to get outside Gerald Davies and cross for a try which McLean converted. The stand-off completed the day's scoring with a penalty goal to make his own contribution 14 points.

J. P. R. WILLIAMS: Despite our dissatisfaction with the referee I must make clear my view that Australia were the better side on the day.

Lest you doubt the strictures of Gerald Davies and myself about the refereeing of Mr Burnett, let me recall one or two prime moments from the provincial game with Queensland (before which he had to be dissuaded from wearing that State's stockings!)

Once, when I queried a decision, he told me: 'I'm a Queenslander, Williams, so I have to look after our boys.'

When Terry Holmes was about to feed a scrummage he was told by the referee, 'It's not your ball, Holmes. It's ours.'

Looking back, such small-mindedness is laughable. But, like Pat Murphy's refereeing years before in New Zealand, it hurt at the time.

11 November 1978 at Cardiff

WALES   12 (4PG)
NEW ZEALAND 13 (1T 3PG)

FACT BOX

J. P. R. Williams captained Wales for the first time.

Wales   J. P. R. Williams (Bridgend, Captain), J. J. Williams (Llanelli), R. W. R. Gravell (Llanelli), S. P. Fenwick (Bridgend), C. F. W. Rees (L. Welsh), W. G. Davies (Cardiff), T. D. Holmes (Cardiff), A. G. Faulkner (Pontypool), R. W. Windsor (Pontypool), G. Price (Pontypool), A. J. Martin (Aberavon), G. A. D. Wheel (Swansea), P. Ringer (Ebbw Vale), D. L. Quinnell (Llanelli), J. Squire (Pontypool).

New Zealand   C. J. Currie, S. S. Wilson, B. J. Robertson, W. J. Osborne, B. G. Williams, O. D. Bruce, D. S. Loveridge, B. R. Johnstone, A. G. Dalton, W. K. Bush, A. M. Haden, F. J. Oliver, L. M. Rutledge, G. A. Seear, G. N. K. Mourie (Captain).
Replacement: B. J. McKechnie for Currie.

SCORERS
Wales   *Pens.* – Gareth Davies (3), Fenwick.
New Zealand   *Try* – Wilson;
Pens. – McKechnie (3).

Referee: R. C. Quittenton (RFU).

GERALD DAVIES: Years earlier I had skippered Wales in an unofficial Test match against Tonga. But this was the first time the honour of captaining my country had been conferred upon me in a full International match. And — sadly — my team was an absolute lash-up!

During the game Graham Price's jaw was fractured in two places by a punch thrown from the Wallaby front row. Donovan fell awkwardly, and suffered the injury to his knee ligaments which kept him out of the game for eighteen months. Gareth Evans, himself Donovan's replacement, pulled out with a depressed fracture of the cheek-bone. J. P. R. Williams went to full-back, but having sent John Richardson of Aberavon RFC on for a first cap in place of Price — a second replacement — the Welsh were obliged to play out time with fourteen men.

J. P. R. WILLIAMS: The 'Hill' at Sydney Oval was quiet for much of the match. Even the most one-eyed Wallaby fan recognized that despite our crippling injury list we were giving the Aussies a real run for their money.

Preferred to Brynmor Williams, Terry Holmes of Cardiff RFC won a first cap, while his club partner Gareth Davies enjoyed a useful half with the boot which yielded a penalty and a dropped goal. His opposite number McLean went one better with two penalties and a dropped goal.

Australia led at half-time, shortly after which the Welsh pack — whose scrummaging on tour had been consistently good — engineered a pushover try for Holmes. The lead was tossed away when Mark Loane was left unmarked at a goal-line throw-in and had only to fall across for an unconverted try. McLean and Davies exchanged more penalty goals before there came the steepling drop kick by the former which effectively clinched the game for Australia.

GERALD DAVIES: I was in a good position and can confirm that it passed a considerable distance outside the posts. There was astonishment, coupled with anger and disappointment, in our ranks when the score was given.

Had it been disallowed we would have won, for soon clever work by our forwards made room for me to cross near the end for an unconverted try. People who saw me throw the ball high in the air after scoring thought I was delighted at equalling Gareth Edwards's record of twenty tries for Wales. In truth, I was simply relieved that the Australian touch-judge had not stuck his flag up. Such was our mistrust of the officials who ran our matches.

Controversy continued to bedevil Wales until the bitter end, yet the tourists might still have won the Second Test had they remained free from injuries. Terry Cobner, Derek Quinnell and Jeff Squire were all unavailable, causing the choice of J. P. R. Williams as a back-row forward, along with Stuart Lane of Cardiff RFC, who had won his first cap as a replacement in the First Test, and newcomer Clive Davis of Newbridge. Swansea's Alun Donovan made his debut at full-back, and Gerald Davies was given the captaincy.

The old firm. Geoff Wheel *(left)* **and Allan Martin out-jumping the Wallabies at a line-out.**

17 June 1978 at Sydney

AUSTRALIA 19 (1T 2DG 3PG)
WALES 17 (2T 1DG 2PG)

FACT BOX

Honoured with the captaincy of Wales for the first time in what was to be his last International appearance, Gerald Davies celebrated by scoring a 20th try and drawing level with record-holder Gareth Edwards.

Australia L. E. Monaghan, P. G. Batch, A. G. Slack, M. Knight, P. J. Crowe, P. E. McLean, R. G. Hauser, S. C. Finnane, P. A. Horton, S. J. Pilecki, D. W. Hillhouse, G. Fay, G. Cornelson, M. E. Loane, A. A. Shaw (Captain).

Wales A. J. Donovan (Swansea), T. G. R. Davies (Cardiff, Captain), S. P. Fenwick (Bridgend), R. W. R. Gravell (Llanelli), J. J. Williams (Llanelli), W. G. Davies (Cardiff), T. D. Holmes (Cardiff), A. G. Faulkner (Pontypool), R. W. Windsor (Pontypool), G. Price (Pontypool), A. J. Martin (Aberavon), G. A. D. Wheel (Swansea), J. P. R. Williams (Bridgend), C. E. Davis (Newbridge), S. M. Lane (Cardiff). *Replacements*: S. J. Richardson (Aberavon) for Graham Price; G. L. Evans (Newport) for Alun Donovan.

SCORERS
Australia *Try* – Loane; *Pens.* – McLean (3); *D.Gs.* – McLean, Monaghan.
Wales *Tries* – Gerald Davies, Holmes; *Pens.* – Gareth Davies (2); *D.G.* – Gareth Davies.

Referee: R. Byers (N.S.W.).

Their victory of 1953 had put Wales 3–1 up over New Zealand in a series stretching back to 1905. Thereafter, however, the All Blacks had won five matches in a row, and on this day they made it six.

BARRY JOHN: Wales also plunged to a third successive defeat at the hands of a Southern Hemisphere nation. This threw into relief our Celtic tendency to look the other way and pretend that nothing disastrous had happened.

Wherever you turned in this era there were Triple Crown and Grand Slam blazers and ties. It was as if wearing these was all that counted. You would never have thought, for example, that Wales were just back from humiliating Test defeats at the hands of the Wallabies.

Gerald Davies and Terry Cobner having followed Gareth Edwards and Phil Bennett into retirement from International rugby, Clive Rees and new cap Paul Ringer of Ebbw Vale RFC were drafted in to face Graham Mourie's All blacks. J. P. R. Williams at last became Wales's captain, with a team that looked experienced enough to give the tourists a run for their money.

It did, and for once it can be stated with certainty that New Zealand were lucky to win. As injury-time was reached they trailed 10–12, at which point referee R. C. Quittenton awarded a penalty for barging against Geoff Wheel 35 metres from the Welsh posts. Considering the prevailing tension, Brian McKechnie (a replacement for the injured Currie) did magnificently to place a winning goal.

Although Wheel was careless enough to brush an opponent's shoulder with his hand — thereby justifying Mr Quittenton's ruling — there seems no doubt that All Black locks Frank Oliver and Andy Haden connived to hoodwink the Englishman. As the throw-in took place both players leaped away from the line-out as if to suggest that they had been shouldered off balance. The bodily contact in the case of Oliver was minimal, in that of Haden non-existent.

J. P. R. WILLIAMS: The All Blacks do not exactly smell of roses to me, but I still admire them a lot. That is why, when I was shown the video-tape of the line-out which cost us the match, I felt sick. If their players could stoop that low to win a game, what was New Zealand rugby coming to?

Defeat in such circumstances was a sorry reward for the Welshmen, whose forwards were inspired by Derek Quinnell to engage top gear at the outset and stay in it for most of the game. For once it was Wales who played the pressure rugby which forced infringements. Bush gave away one penalty. Then Currie was hurt in a heavy tackle by Fenwick, lay on the ball unable to move, conceded a penalty, and was helped away to the medical room. Finally Brian Williams tripped his opposite number, J. J. Williams. Gareth Davies (twice) and Fenwick were the Welsh kickers who built up a 9–0 lead.

The tourists struck back with a gem of a try. Their pack drove into the Welsh 22-area, releasing possession which was beautifully exploited by Bill Osborne. The centre made as if to break, checking

the Welsh defenders momentarily, before placing a perfect kick-ahead for Stu Wilson. The wing won a thrilling race to touch down.

Gareth Davies kicked another penalty for Wales, and although McKechnie replied with two more the home side looked strong enough to retain their two-point lead. The All Blacks weathered a stern battering, however, and McKechnie's stunning blow just before no-side gave them the spoils.

Replacement Brian McKechnie seals Wales's fate with a perfectly-judged injury-time penalty.

J. P. R. WILLIAMS: Losing this game, my first as Wales skipper, was unquestionably the biggest disappointment of my career. To keep cool during a TV interview as I left the field was, I think, a considerable diplomatic achievement!

BARRY JOHN: My Press box contribution to the Haden–Oliver line-out fiasco was to shout, 'Hollywood!' I felt great anger and sadness that a fine game should end on such a note.

MATCH 60

20 January 1979 at Murrayfield
SCOTLAND 13 (1T 3PG)
WALES 19 (1G 1T 3PG)

Elgan Rees, a try-scorer, and Graham Price: all smiles after the friendly gust of icy wind.

FACT BOX

Scotland A. R. Irvine, K. W. Robertson, J. M. Renwick, I. R. McGeechan (Captain), B. H. Hay, J. Y. Rutherford, A. J. M. Lawson, J. McLauchlan, C. T. Deans, R. F. Cunningham, A. J. Tomes, A. F. McHarg, M. A. Biggar, I. K. Lambie, G. Dickson.

Wales J. P. R. Williams (Bridgend, Captain), H. E. Rees (Neath), S. P. Fenwick (Bridgend), R. W. R. Gravell (Llanelli), J. J. Williams (Llanelli), W. G. Davies (Cardiff), T. D. Holmes (Cardiff), A. G. Faulkner (Pontypool), R. W. Windsor (Pontypool), G. Price (Pontypool), A. J. Martin (Aberavon), G. A. D. Wheel (Swansea), P. Ringer (Llanelli), D. L. Quinnell (Llanelli), J. Squire (Pontypool).

SCORERS
Scotland *Try* – Irvine; *Pens.* – Irvine (3).
Wales *Tries* – Holmes, Rees; *Con.* – Fenwick; *Pens.* – Fenwick (3).

Referee: F. Palmade (FRF).

Bouncing back after three successive defeats, Wales achieved lift-off in defence of their European title. A Scottish side which displayed more courage than cohesion was first contained and then subdued by a granite-hard forward effort, of which Derek Quinnell was an outstanding controller.

MERVYN DAVIES: By this time, as he had also shown against New Zealand, Derek had become a great leader of men. As a player I wish he had concentrated on one position in order to fulfil his true potential. In the end he fell some way short of this through appearing at number 8 and flanker. Lock was his best place.

Elgan Rees of Neath RFC was the sole new cap in a Welsh XV which made numerous numb-fingered mistakes in the freezing conditions and allowed Scotland to build a substantial lead. Andy Irvine cancelled out an early penalty by Steve Fenwick and

then kicked his country in front before playing a big part in the afternoon's most spectacular move.

Seizing upon a sloppy clearance by Gareth Davies, he beat Rees and sprinted infield to the Welsh 10-metre line, where the running was taken up by Ian McGeechan and Alan Tomes. Astonishingly, Irvine materialized again outside the pair to

accept a scoring pass, crossing just too far out for his own conversion attempt. He added a penalty goal after thirty-six minutes.

J. P. R. WILLIAMS: Penalties by Steve Fenwick on each side of the interval kept us in the hunt and provided encouragement for a great fight-back, which was given momentum by Elgan Rees's try.

I took a pass inside Scotland's 22-area from Steve Fenwick and, as the cover moved up, took the only available course of action and chipped the ball towards the corner flag. As luck would have it a friendly gust of icy wind brought it down neatly into the hands of our unmarked wing! His try tied the score.

Although the Welsh eight — with Jeff Squire demonstrating what a competitive forward he had become — continued to hold the whip-hand, Scotland defended bravely. There were only minutes left for play when their resistance cracked under a particularly strong thrust by the front five of the Welsh pack — Price, Faulkner, Windsor, Martin and Wheel. Forcing the Scottish forwards back across their own goal-line, they gave Quinnell and Terry Holmes the chance to drop upon the ball simultaneously for a try which Fenwick converted. Class and skill had won the day, but Scotland had died bravely.

MATCH 61

3 February 1979 at Cardiff
WALES 24 (2G 4PG)
IRELAND 21 (2G 3PG)

Patterson probes for Ireland, and the Welsh defence closes ranks. From the Press Box Barry John could see that the Golden Age was drawing to a close.

This was a hard-earned victory for Wales. Each side scored two converted tries, but Steve Fenwick kicked one more penalty goal than Tony Ward — to give his country a three-point margin of success.

BARRY JOHN: Although there was a brief revival against England in March it was in this game (and the previous one against Scotland) that I saw signs which pointed to the close of our Golden Age.

Winning margins were getting narrower. Victory often seemed dependent on the whims of referees and the penalty kicks at goal they awarded. Earlier in the decade such considerations had not bothered Welsh teams.

Mistakes by the home pack in the game's early stages allowed Ward to secure a 6–0 lead for Ireland with two well-judged penalties. After twenty-five minutes, however, Gareth Davies hoisted a towering up-and-under towards the visitors' line, where, closing ferociously upon Dick Spring, his team-mates caused the full-back to miss his catch. As the ball ran loose across the goal-line Allan Martin threw himself full length for a first International try. Fenwick converted, and helped

himself to two penalties before the interval, by which time Ward had completed a hat-trick for the Irish.

Although the departure of Geoff Wheel with a pinched shoulder nerve caused concern in the Welsh camp, a reshuffled back row into which Stuart Lane had been drafted as a replacement quickly made Fergus Slattery's men pay for slipshod work on their goal-line. Colin Patterson misdirected his pass to Ward, and Paul Ringer hurtled through to score for Wales.

PHIL BENNETT: Paul was one of a dying breed — flankers who flew off a scrum to take out the opposing stand-off half and crowd the midfield. His speed and anticipation allowed his stand-off half to stay back and cover across behind the three-quarters.

Fenwick sent over the conversion, and added another penalty goal a quarter of an hour after half-time. But then Ireland launched the offensive which nearly prevented a home victory. Centres McNaughton and McKibbin came pounding through the midfield to create trouble for defender J. J. Williams. A good second-phase ball allowed Ward to place a perfect diagonal kick away to Freddie McLennan's wing, and the pint-sized Wanderer crossed the line with three defenders round his neck. Ward converted the try, as well as Ireland's final score by Patterson.

But in the meantime Fenwick had made the match safe for Wales with a penalty goal which took his personal tally of points in International matches beyond the 100 mark.

17 February 1979 at Parc des Princes
FRANCE 14 (2T 2PG)
WALES 13 (1T 3PG)

Bertranne, Belascain and Rives came close to scoring. Finally, full-back Aguirre arrowed his way down the blind side and slipped the fair-haired Gourdon in for an unconverted try.

J. P. R. WILLIAMS: J. J. Williams appeared to have Gourdon covered, but made the mistake of turning inside towards Aguirre, whom I was ready to tackle. Once the pass had been given, J.J. could not regain sufficient speed to halt Gourdon.

FACT BOX

France J-M. Aguirre, J-F. Gourdon, R. Bertranne, C. Belascain, G. Noves, A. Caussade, J. Gallion, A. Vaquerin, A. Paco, R. Paparemborde, A. Maleig, F. Haget, J-L. Joinel, A. Guilbert, J-P. Rives (Captain).

Wales J. P. R. Williams (Bridgend, Captain), H. E. Rees (Neath), D. S. Richards (Swansea), S. P. Fenwick (Bridgend), J. J. Williams (Llanelli), W. G. Davies (Cardiff), T. D. Holmes (Cardiff), A. G. Faulkner (Pontypool), R. W. Windsor (Pontypool), G. Price (Pontypool), A. J. Martin (Aberavon), B. G. Clegg (Swansea), J. Squire (Pontypool), D. L. Quinnell (Llanelli), P. Ringer (Llanelli).

SCORERS
France *Tries* – Gourdon (2);
Pens. – Aguirre (2).
Wales *Try* – Holmes; *Pen.* – Fenwick (3).

Referee: D. I. H. Burnett (IRFU).

Cardiff's Terry Holmes – a worthy sucessor in the Welsh XV to the great Gareth Edwards.

Paris again proved an insurmountable hurdle for a Welsh side which had begun to entertain hopes of another Grand Slam, and France's victory was more comfortable than the score suggests.

With Geoff Wheel still unfit, Barry Clegg, a Swansea RFC clubmate, won a first cap, as did another Swansea player, David Richards, who had been an outstanding schoolboy stand-off half. First choice in the position because of his superior line-kicking was Gareth Davies, but deciding that the gifts of Richards could no longer be ignored, the selectors picked him to partner Fenwick in the centre. Out went Ray Gravell, whose direct methods seemed for the time being to have become too predictable.

After a Fenwick penalty goal against the run of play had put Wales ahead the French swept back to the visitors' 22-area, where in quick succession

A break into French territory by Elgan Rees was ended by a high tackle, and although Fenwick struck the penalty attempt wide, Wales forced their opponents back to their goal-line. Here, following a line-out at which the defenders were careless, Bobby Windsor set up a maul from which Terry Holmes scored an unconverted try. By half-time, however, after visiting midfield players had strayed offside, Aguirre had levelled the scores with a penalty goal.

He put over another soon afterwards, to which Fenwick promptly replied. Then France took the lead for the third and last time. Seizing a loose clearance, Noves made a spectacular cross-field burst towards the French right, where once more Gourdon eluded his markers to get through for a try

which remained unconverted. There were still eighteen minutes of play left when Fenwick kicked his third penalty goal; and Wales began moving the ball frenziedly in their efforts to nose ahead again.

J. P. R. WILLIAMS: The French took everything we could throw at them, and in reality were so much better than us on the day that it is amazing how closely we ran them. A few minutes from full time Steve Fenwick took a long-range shot at goal which could have won us the match — but defeat would have been a terrible injustice to our opponents.

At the close the home team, demonstrably the stronger, were camped securely in their opponents' 22-area.

17 March 1979 at Cardiff

WALES 27 (2G 3T 1DG)
ENGLAND 3 (1PG)

An early probe for England by scrum half Peter Kingston. But Wales were to score five tries.

FACT BOX

J. P. R. Williams announced his retirement at the end of a season in which he led Wales not only to their 21st outright Five Nations Championship title but also to an amazing fourth Triple Crown in successive seasons – a record which may never be equalled.

Wales J. P. R. Williams (Bridgend, Captain), H. E. Rees (Neath), D. S. Richards (Swansea), S. P. Fenwick (Bridgend), J. J. Williams (Llanelli), W. G. Davies (Cardiff), T. D. Holmes (Cardiff), S. J. Richardson (Aberavon), A. J. Phillips (Cardiff), G. Price (Pontypool), A. J. Martin (Aberavon), M. G. Roberts (L. Welsh), J. Squire (Pontypool), D. L. Quinnell (Llanelli), P. Ringer (Llanelli).
Replacement: C. Griffiths (Llanelli) for J.P.R.

England A. J. Hignell, P. J. Squires, R. M. Cardus, P. W. Dodge, M. A. C. Slemen, W. N. Bennett, P. Kingston, C. Smart, P. J. Wheeler, G. S. Pearce, W. B. Beaumont (Captain), N. E. Horton, A. Neary, J. P. Scott, M. Rafter.

SCORERS
Wales *Tries* – Richards, Ringer, Roberts, Rees, J. J. Williams; *Cons.* – Martin, Fenwick; *D.G.* – Davies.
England *Pen.* – Bennett.

Referee J. P. Bonnet (FRF).

By beating France at Twickenham a fortnight earlier England had made it possible for Wales to become Champions of the Five Nations for a second year running. The chance was seized avidly, and the visitors were sent packing over the Severn Bridge after their biggest hiding in Cardiff for a decade.

With John Richardson and Mike Roberts in for Faulkner and Clegg, Wales began with spirit, Gareth Davies dropping a goal. Soon good work at a line-out by Derek Quinnell and Allan Martin, with consequent rapid possession, encouraged J. P. R.

Williams to race alongside the centres and send David Richards speeding in for a great try. England hit back with a Neil Bennett penalty.

But now the golden age of world-class players drew to its close. After bravely halting an England attack, skipper J.P.R. was forced to leave the field with blood pouring from a leg-wound. As one, the 50,000 crowd saluted him.

J. P. R. WILLIAMS: The last thing I wanted was to leave the fray with England pressing hard. But the gash — which needed 14 stitches — meant that I could do no more than hobble.

GARETH EDWARDS: Fate seemed to have played J.P.R. — the Warrior supreme — an unkind trick in what we all thought would be his last International match. Compared to some of the wounds he had suffered in his time, this was just a nick. Even when Clive Griffiths of Llanelli came on as replacement I still could not accept that the captain would not be returning. He always seemed indestructible.

Lock Mike Roberts now supplied the inspiration which Wales needed. At a line-out beside England's corner flag he evaded Bill Beaumont and crashed over for a try which prompted his team-mates to run riot. Soon Steve Fenwick gave intelligent support to a thrilling break by J. J. Williams, and was able to provide Paul Ringer with a scoring pass. Back in the midfield Fenwick was again on hand when Elgan Rees ran into trouble, retrieving a loose ball and feeding Richards. The young centre sent a perfectly timed pass to J.J., who reached the corner.

As the match entered injury time young Clive Griffiths picked up an awkward pass and put in the touch-line dash which led to the fifth Welsh try, touched down by Rees. Conversions by Fenwick and Martin contributed to a final total of 27 points.

GARETH EDWARDS: A great player leaves the scene — and scarcely has there been time to blink before his successor is there, staking a new claim to greatness.

It was uncanny. J.P.R. had gone; and not in the next

season, not in the next match, but in the next *moment* we beheld Clive Griffiths opening a new era.

J. P. R. WILLIAMS: Feeling considerable pride, I sat in the Committee Box and watched my team clinch the match and the Five Nations' title. I felt especially happy for Derek Quinnell, whom I had left in charge on the field, and Mike Roberts, brought back to neutralize the Beaumont threat.

It had been a great thrill to lead Wales. And it's nice to be on the list of Championship captains.

Championship Table 1978–79

	P	W	D	L	PF	PA	Pts
WALES (1)	4	3	0	1	83	51	6
FRANCE (2)	4	2	1	1	50	46	5
IRELAND (4)	4	1	2	1	53	51	4
ENGLAND (3)	4	1	1	2	24	52	3
SCOTLAND (5)	4	0	2	2	48	48	2

Numbers in brackets indicate last season's positions.

Welsh results during the Golden Era

Played 63: Won 38, Drawn 5, Lost 20, Points For 1005, Points Against 683

Grand Slams (3): 1970–71, 1975–76, 1977–78

Triple Crowns (6): 1968–69, 1970–71, 1975–76, 1976–77, 1977–78, 1978–79

Championship Titles: 1968–69, 1969–70 (*with France*), 1970–71, 1971–72, 1972–73 (*five-way tie*), 1974–75, 1975–76, 1977–78, 1978–79

POSTSCRIPT

To the surprise and delight of his admirers J. P. R. Williams emerged from retirement at the beginning of the 1980–81 season and declared himself available for International rugby. The age of the Superstars thus enjoyed a brief Indian summer.

J. P. R. WILLIAMS: Several factors tempted me back. It was Wales's centenary season, with unique celebration matches in the offing. New Zealand were due at the Arms Park for a Test match in November. Wales seemed short of likely lads for the full-back position.

So I decided to give it a go, and although we lost heavily to the All Blacks I proved to myself that I could make a successful comeback.

It was a bonus to take part in the Wales–England v. Scotland–Ireland match, and gave me the honour of being the only man to have played in the equivalent Centenary fixtures of all four Home Countries.

In January came an appearance against England which took me ahead of Gareth Edwards as the most capped Welsh player of all time. Appropriately I finished on the winning side against the visitors for the eleventh consecutive time, having never been a loser against them.

After my fifty-fifth appearance, in another of the Murrayfield disasters with which Wales's record is sprinkled, I was dropped. In the end, it didn't seem important: my feeling was that a majority of Welsh supporters would still have preferred me in the National XV for another match or two — and that it was the selectors who were out of step.

ACKNOWLEDGMENTS

The publishers and author wish to thank the following sources for permission to reproduce the photographs: Western Mail and Echo 2–3, 10–11, 12–13, 14–15, 18–19, 20–1, 22–3, 24–5, 27, 28–9, 32–3, 34, 35, 36–7, 39, 43, 45, 54–5, 58–9, 61, 72–3, 91, 97, 100, 101, 106, 111, 113, 121, 122, 126–7, 129, 130, 131, 133, 135, 138–9, 142–3; Colorsport 1, 4, 6, 8–9, 17, 38, 40–1, 51, 53, 62–3, 65, 66–7, 68, 69, 71, 75, 77, 78–9, 82–3, 85, 87, 88–9, 92–3, 95, 103, 104–5, 107, 108–9, 115, 117, 120–1, 124–5, 136–7, 140–1; Sport and General 31, 56–7; Peter Stuart 49; The Scotsman 80–1.